Training for decent work

Trazos de la ***Formación***

Cover: Butcher counter, miniature 15th century, National Library, Paris

Training for decent work

International Labour Office

CINTERFOR

CINTERFOR
Training for decent work. Montevideo : Cinterfor, 2001.
104 p.   (Trazos de la Formación, 12)

Incluye bibliografía
ISBN 92-9088-125-9

/FORMACIÓN PROFESIONAL/ /TRABAJO/ /IGUALDAD DE OPOR-TUNIDADES/ /CONCERTACIÓN SOCIAL/ /POLÍTICA DE EMPLEO/ /PUB CINTERFOR/

ILO publications can be obtained through major booksellers or ILO local offices in many countries, or direct from ILO Publications, International Labour Office, CH 1211 Geneva 22, Switzerland. Catalogues or lists of new publications are available free of charge from the above address, or by e-mail to: pubvente@ilo.org. Web site: www.ilo.org/publns

The Inter-American Research and Documentation Centre on Vocational Training (Cinterfor/ILO) is an ILO technical service, set up in 1964 with the aim of encouraging and coordinating the action of the Latin American and Caribbean institutes, organisations and agencies involved in vocational training.

The Centre publications can be obtained through ILO local offices in many countries, or direct from Cinterfor/ILO, Casilla de correo 1761, e-mail: dirmvd@cinterfor.org.uy. Fax 902 1305, Montevideo, Uruguay

Web site: www.cinterfor.org.uy

Hecho el depósito legal núm. 322.618/2001   Printed in Cinterfor/ILO

TABLE OF CONTENTS

NOTE

One of the concerns of the ILO is the use of language that may not imply unjustified discrimination between men and women. In Spanish, however, this raises problems of different kinds, about which consensus has not yet been reached.

In the Spanish original, therefore, the generic masculine was used in all cases, to avoid spelling overloading, on the understanding that all instances always represent both sexes.

INTRODUCTION

Work is a fundamental aspect in the life of individuals. It is not only a form of sustenance and satisfaction of the basic needs of human beings; it is also vehicle for persons to reassert their own dignity, occupy a productive place and feel useful to society and their family.

Despite the dizzying technological transformations undergone by the way in which men and women produce, the significance of work in the lives of people has not changed. The concern to get a job and develop the skills necessary for keeping it, is still in the forefront of the preoccupations of millions upon millions of persons, whatever the degree of development of their respective societies and the cultural aspects differentiating them.

But people do not just want a trade enabling them to survive in constant anxiety. They want decent work, in adequate conditions enabling them to enjoy a minimum of social protection. They want jobs guaranteeing all those who work their fundamental rights, building on that respect a transparent social dialogue. They want work to be an instrument for their permanent betterment, a place for developing their capabilities, enabling them to compete in the market and keep abreast with technological qualifications.

But just as I said in my Report to the International Labour Conference in June 2001, entitled *Reducing the Deficit of Decent Work: a global challenge,* we are still far from complying with people's aspirations, and the global shortage of decent work is the most arduous task we have to tackle at this moment. Insufficient, poor quality employment, inadequate social protection, the waiving of labour rights and an imperfect social dialogue, are signs indicating the deep breach that exists between the reality in which men and women have to toil, and the expectations people have of a better life.

Consequently, efforts have to be redoubled to bring down that deficit. Not only will power is required but also an approach systematically reconciling social and economic goals, both at local, national and world level. It is also necessary for policies to be analysed from the angle of their concrete effect on the life of individuals and their families.

7

Globalisation has exacerbated the need to compete in order to become success-fully established in the different markets. This requirement for competitiveness forces enterprises to turn into centres of creativity and efficiency if they want to survive. It also necessitates that workers be permanently attuned with the techno-logical evolution of their work, so that they may themselves be more creative and efficient. Decent work is the frame wherein both needs can be met through voca-tional training.

Training and the development of workers' skills and competencies is a crucial dimension of decent work. Economic interests, social imperatives and the right of working persons to dignity – all of them inherent in the notion of decent work – come together in it in a more evident manner than elsewhere. For that reason, vocational training has special prominence on the ILO agenda.

The quality of the social and human capital, denoted by the accumulated compe-tencies of its labour force, is what makes it possible for a society to grow and develop along loftier channels, that is to say, through a constant increase of pro-ductivity on the basis of an ever greater intellectual worth. It is in turn the dominant element for augmenting the economic and social value of the human factor in the production equation, and the recognition it may be granted in the distribution of its merits. The investment a society may make in the qualification, retraining and constant improvement of its labour force is a precondition for its capacity to fit into a globalised economy. The global integration of markets is a cause of convulsion in employment, with a consequent loss of work posts in some sectors, and the creation of others in other sectors. This calls for a deliberate proactive policy of skills development, capable of countering such pressures, enabling workers to benefit from new opportunities, and allowing enterprises to react in time and take advantage of new niches.

It is almost self-evident to say that the quality of human resources is a strategic factor for the survival and development of enterprises. Nevertheless, this has nowa-days a dramatic priority and is therefore an essential factor in the creation and maintenance of good quality jobs. Caught in the relentless race towards competi-tiveness, and faced with the challenges of adaptation and creativity in increasingly complex and demanding markets, each company needs to have a contingent of trained workers, capable of learning and adapting not only to new occupational profiles but to new forms of labour organisation and changing production require-ments. Training by competencies is also essential for the creation of new enter-prises and to increase the productivity and profitability of small and medium firms whose most cherished capital is their qualified personnel. I is also the instrument that can ensure the stability, productivity and income of the workers that survive in the informal sector, in low-income traditional activities or in precarious, unprotected jobs that lack the comparative advantage of a training capital.

8

For each man or woman wishing to secure a decent job, his or her own occupational training is the starting point to raise their employability conditions, in an economy characterised by constant pressure towards the increase of productivity, that imposes growing demands in the field of technology and knowledge. It also offers the best credentials to opt for a quality job, i.e. a productive, satisfactory, well remunerated job, performed in acceptable working conditions and rewarded by fundamental labour rights. Besides, it constitutes the most effective passport for accessing work opportunities, the most efficient protection against discrimination and exclusion in the labour market and the most useful safeguard in times of readjustment and recycling to face the restructuring of productive activities.

Vocational training is an integral and unavoidable part of the ILO agenda to reduce the deficit of decent work in the world. It is dynamically co-ordinated into a virtuous spiral of more and better jobs, respect of the rights an dignity of workers, and social and economic security and protection. Furthermore, it has proved to be a propitious environment for dialogue, negotiation and agreement among the leading players in the realm of labour, underlining the positive contribution of the labour force to growth and prosperity. To sum up, it lies at the core of an overall agenda for decent work, as a privileged strategy for growth, innovation, competitiveness. social inclusion, the eradication of poverty and achievement of the occupational and personal fulfilment of all working men and women.

I am therefore pleased to urge the vocational training institutions of he ILO Member States of the Americas and Spain, to continue deploying their efforts to develop the human and occupational abilities of today's and tomorrow's workers, and I invite them, through Cinterfor, to maintain close co-operation ties with the ILO in the pursuit of training of a kind that may lead to decent work.

JUAN SOMAVÍA
Director General ILO

9

FOREWORD

This book has been envisaged as a contribution to defining the concept of decent work and promoting its achievement, as objectives adopted by the International Labour Organisation. It approaches its task from the particular viewpoint of the prospects and practices of the vocational training institutions of the Latin American and Caribbean Region.

Insofar as they are a fundamental right of current or potential workers, vocational education and training are unavoidable components of any dignified job, especially in the midst of technological progress and the society of knowledge. As an instrument for productivity and competitiveness, they are a prerequisite for the economic efficiency that generates quality employment. As providers of workers' qualifications, they are a precondition for access to work and permanence in it. For those reasons training is part of the concept of decent work and an essential element of any action aimed at attaining it. We may assert that there is no decent work without vocational training.

Such is the thesis developed in this volume, which also singles out the most interesting experiences carried out by the training bodies of the Region along the lines of decent work.

It also reflects – with due adaptation and adjustment – Reference Document N° 1 of the 35th Meeting of the Cinterfor/ILO Technical Committee, held at Brasilia on 30th August and 1st September 2001. With its publication, our Centre hopes to have made a significant contribution to the ILO's central objectives. This book was the result of the joint effort of the Centre's technical staff under the co-ordination of Oscar Ermida Uriarte and Fernando Casanova.

PEDRO DANIEL WEINBERG
Director, Cinterfor/ILO

I
DECENT WORK AND TRAINING

1.   Although the notion of *decent work,* proposed by the Director General of the ILO in his first Report to the International Labour Conference[1], may be seen as an objective or purpose[2] devoid of technical content, it can also be considered as an *integrating concept* bringing together and co-ordinating diverse aims, values and policies[3], or as a "dynamic concept, whose content evolves with the social and economic progress of a given country".[4]

In any case, it appears that on the one hand we have here a notion whose content had not been altogether defined – and had therefore to be 'fleshed out'[5] - and on the other that such concept, though ill defined, had an indisputable ethical content or significance[6]: promoting decent work presupposes the adoption of a clear-cut attitude in favour of the dignity of man.

In that respect, this obviously coincides with concerns that previously justified various efforts to include value judgements in the study of industrial relations, which made it possible to "consider a given system as ethically acceptable"[7].

---

[1]   OIT, *Trabajo decente,* Memoria del Director General a la 87ª Reunión de la Conferencia Internacional del Trabajo, Ginebra, 1999.

[2]   STANDING, Guy, *Modes of control: a labour status approach to decent work.*ILO. Geneva, Nov. 2000, (mimeographed document). p. 1.

[3]   ILO, *Proposal for a Decent Work Pilot Programme (DW/PP),* Geneva, 10 Oct, 2000, mimeographed as "rough copy", p. 2.

[4]   OIT, *Trabajo decente para la mujer. Una propuesta de la OIT para acelerar la puesta en práctica de la Plataforma de Acción de Pekin,* Oficina para la Igualdad de Género, mimeographed n/d, p. 10.

[5]   The ILO has charged the International Institute for Labour Studies (IILS) with drawing up a paradigm of decent work and has set up a special working group for that purpose (*cf.* N° 7 below).

[6]   SOMAVÍA, Juan, *Discurso del 1° de Mayo de 2000 en presencia del Papa Juan Pablo II.* press communiqué ILO/ 00/15. Mentions human dignity on several occasions, and the conscious exercise of a moral sense.

[7]   In that order, LOCKE, Richard, KOCHAN, Thomas, and PIORE, Michael, *Replanteamiento del estudio comparado en las relaciones laborales: enseñanzas de una investigación internacional,* Revista Internacional del Trabajo, Ginebra 1995, vol. 114 N° 2, p. 180; ERMIDA URIARTE, Oscar, *Relaciones laborales, nuevas variables e indicadores,* en Revista Judicatura, Montevideo 1999, N° 40, pp. 56 y 63; GRUPO BOLOGNA/CASTILLA–LA MANCHA, SECRETARÍA PRO-TÉMPORE, *Concepto y medición del trabajo decente,* mimeographed, Montevideo 2001, paras. 1 and 5.

2.   On the other hand, the importance of vocational training is increasingly recognised. It is proclaimed a fundamental right of workers, but consensus grows about the fact that the fast track to economic competitiveness is based on added value, on quality and on the so-called "human capital". Simultaneously, training is accepted as a factor for employability, and as such it becomes a central element in employment policies. All of which is reinforced by the dissemination of information technologies and the advent of the society of knowledge.

In such circumstances it seems necessary –almost unavoidable– to consider the relationship between training and decent work. The present document endeavours to provide some insights into that.

3.   Based on the above, we shall now proceed to analyse firstly the definitions so far made, sketched or hinted at of the so-called *decent work* within the ILO. Secondly, we shall study the role of vocational training in attaining that goal. And thirdly, we shall refer to decent work and the ILO strategic objectives. Subsequently, in the body of the document –divided into four parts – we shall analyse the role of vocational training in fulfilling each one of the objectives that are considered to be components of decent work: labour rights, employment, social protection and social dialogue.

DEFINITION OF DECENT WORK

4.   A first approximation to the meaning of the expression "decent work" may be the purely grammatical approach, which does not always coincide with technical concepts. Nevertheless, in this case the literal sense of "decent work" is particularly appropriate, at least in Spanish and in English.

In effect, in English one of the first acceptations of the word decent is "satisfactory; of an acceptable standard". One of the dictionaries looked up provides the following example: "All she wants is a decent job with decent wages"[8]. And in Spanish the third acceptation for the word "decente" is "of good quality and in sufficient quantity"[9]. Which is evidence that, even in common language, a decent job is at least *sufficient in quality and quantity.*

---

[8]   *Oxford Wordplace Dictionary,* Oxford, 1993, p. 165. *cf. also* EGGER, Philippe, and SENGENBERGER, Werner, *Decent Work Issues and Policies, Decent work Pilot Programme, Note 1. http://www.ilo.org.*

[9]   REAL ACADEMIA ESPAÑOLA, *Diccionario de la lengua española,* 21ª ed., Madrid 1992. *Cf.* BARRETTO GHIONE, Hugo, *Diálogo social y formación: una perspectiva desde los países del Mercosur y México,* Serie Aportes para el Diálogo social y la Formación, N° 7, Cinterfor/OIT, Montevideo 2001, p. 9.

5.   As said earlier, the first express and formal mention of the expression decent work in the ILO and in labour science appears to have occurred in the Director General's Report to the International Labour Conference in 1999, which bears that title. An initial definition is included there: productive work under conditions of freedom equity, security and dignity, in which rights are protected and adequate remuneration and social coverage are provided[10].

Consequently in this first -preliminary- formulation, decent work was characterised by the following components: a) productive work; b) protection of rights; c) adequate pay; and d) social protection. According to what the same document went on to say, a fifth essential element would have to be added: e) tripartite approach and social dialogue[11].

Apart from the above, the document under review mentions the decision of linking that preliminary notion of decent work to the four strategic objectives set for the 2000-2001 ILO programme, which would supposedly lead to decent work. They are: a) the promotion of labour rights; b) the promotion of employment; c) social protection for vulnerable situations; and d) the promotion of social dialogue[12].

6.   In a regional document issued shortly afterwards, decent work is described as a good quality job respecting the rights of workers and affording them some form of social protection[13]. Some differences are worth noting: the idea of productive work is here replaced by that of good quality employment; there is no reference to adequate remuneration (which, however, could be implicit in the *good quality* adjective), to tripartism or social dialogue, although that also might pertain to the respect for the rights of workers.

Features that do not figure in the definition proposed by this document, are mentioned and developed subsequently, and include elements of interest like vocational training[14]

7.   Subsequently, in the first global report on follow-up procedures to the ILO Declaration on Fundamental Labour Principles and Rights (1998), on the subject of trade union freedom and collective bargaining, union freedom is closely related to decent work, and considered a precondition for it.

---

[10]   OIT, *Trabajo decente,* cit., p.15.
[11]   Ditto. pp. 15-16.
[12]   Ditto, pp. 4-5.
[13]   OIT, *Trabajo decente y protección para todos.Prioridad de las Américas.* Report of the Regional Director to the 14th Regional Meeting of ILO Member States of the Americas, Lima, Peru. 1999, p.II.
[14]   See below, Nos. 10. 11 and 12.

In fact, the document *begins* by underlining "the crucial role of trade union freedom and collective bargaining to achieve decent work"[15], a concept that is subsequently reiterated[16].

8. In other papers, the ILO Director General referred to concepts of a similar nature, underscoring some elements, adding others.

For instance, the statement that "by decent work we understand labour in conditions of freedom, equity, safety and human dignity"[17]. New meaningful concepts are included, such as *safety* which, as we shall see, has been growing in importance in the definition of decent work, as well as *equity* and *human dignity,* that are closely linked to the already mentioned ethical content of the idea.

Another definition by the ILO Director General himself is that of decent work as productive toil in which rights are respected, safety and protection are provided, as well as the possibility to take part in all decisions that may affect workers[18]. In this case the idea of occupational safety and the need for workers' participation are foremost.

9. As mentioned earlier, the International Institute of Labour Studies (IILS) was asked to draw up a paradigm of decent work and formulate strategies for its dissemination and promotion. The first official documents issued by the IILS after this mandate include some comments that are worth noting.

On the one hand, the mandate says that the Institute's central task will now be "to create a paradigm of decent work" and endow it with a "theoretical structure"[19]. On the other hand, the Institute also relates this as yet ill defined concept of decent work to four of the ILO strategic objectives for 2000-2001, singling them out as its "four basic components"[20], and adding that decent work is not just the sum of these supposed components, but the result of their interaction [21].

---

[15] OIT, *Su voz en el trabajo. Informe global con arreglo al seguimiento-de la Declaración de la OIT relativa a los principios y derechos fundamentales en el trabajo,* Ginebra, 2000, p. VII.
[16] Ditto, p. 2.
[17] SOMAVÍA, Juan, *Un trabajo decente para todos en una econocmía globalizada: una perspectiva de la OIT,* document submitted to the Third WTO Ministerial Meeting (30 Nov. 3 Dec. 1999), http://www.ilo.org. and included in SOMAVÍA, Juan, Perspectives on decent work, ILO, Geneva 2000, p.1 and following pp. (this publication includes several of the documents by the ILO Director General that are quoted in this paper).
[18] SOMAVÍA, Juan, *Introduction* in "Globalising Europe. Decent work in the information economy. Report of the Director General". Sixth European Regional Meeting, ILO, Geneva 2000, vol I, p. X.
[19] IIEL, *Informe del Director,* Ginebra 2000, para. 9.
[20] Ditto, paras. 14-15. This idea is picked up by the Informe de la 42ª Reunión de la Junta Directiva del Instituto. (GB 279/17, 279th M.) Ginebra, 2000, para. 4.
[21] Ditto.

Besides, the Institute's Programme and Budget for 2000-2001 includes two interesting notions. One is that "the concept of decent work brings together a number of matters that have been the ILO's concern since its origins"[22]. Another one, that "decent work refers both to quality and to quantity"[23].

10.   The Report of the Director General to the 89th Meeting of the International Labour Conference reaffirms that decent work is an integrative concept, in which it is necessary to combine aspects pertaining to rights, employment, protection and all-inclusive dialogue.[24] It further states that it constitutes a goal, a framework for defining policies and action, a method of organising activities and programmes, and a springboard for association with other entities[25].

11.   As a necessarily preliminary and provisional conclusion, we may say that decent work is a concept that is being fashioned out; it is integrative and has a deep ethical content.

We may also add that within the ILO, the following characteristics have been attributed to it:

- it is productive and secure work;
- it ensures respect of labour rights;
- it provides an adequate income;
- it offers social protection;
- it includes social dialogue, union freedom, collective bargaining and participation.

Employment security is highlighted in some of the already mentioned documents of the Director General, but it is also mentioned in one of the technical studies, which states that "decent work implies security"[26]. It is obvious that occupational safety, which forms part of the quality of employment -also required-, calls for certain continuity or stability in the work relationship, and is at present closely linked with vocational training. But as we shall see below, this tends to become an essential component of the concept of decent work for other reasons, and may even be considered to be a prerequisite for it. The second part of this paper focuses on those aspects.

---

[22]   IIEL, *Programa y presupuesto para 2000-2001*, Ginebra, 2000, para. 32.
[23]   Ditto, para. 34.
[24]   *Reducir el déficit de trabajo decente. Un desafío Global.* Informe del Director General, OIT, 89ª Reunión de la Conferencia Internacional del Trabajo, Ginebra, 2000, para. 3.5.
[25]   Ditto. para. 1.1.
[26]   STAN DING, Guy, Op. cit. p. 39.

THE ROLE OF VOCATIONAL TRAINING IN CONNECTION WITH DECENT WORK

12.   Vocational training is currently considered to be a *fundamental right* of workers -recognised as such in numerous Pacts and Declarations of human rights, as well as by an increasing number of Constitutions. At the same time it is an *economic instrument* that is part of employment policies and of the productivity and competitiveness strategies of enterprises. All this, combined with the fact that in the *society of knowledge* the role of education, training and lifelong learning is essential, makes it evident that nowadays it is impossible to aim at decent work without vocational training.

Additionally, vocational training is closely related to the features or elements that the ILO deems to be essential components of decent work:

- *equality or non-discrimination* increasingly depends on access to education and vocational training, as well as to ongoing training[27];
- the importance of training for the *employability* of workers, as well as for their adaptability and possibilities of retaining a job, hardly needs justification[28];
- the link of training to *social protection* has been underscored by European trade unions and reflected in ILO documents as "the need to promote ongoing education for those who risk exclusion, in view of the growth of the society of information, as well as for older workers"[29];
- the ever closer tie between *social dialogue* and training has been highlighted and turned into an ILO mandate, in the Resolution on the development of human resources adopted by the International Labour Conference of 2000[30].

In some of the documents quoted above vocational training has been included - sometimes under the guise of "development of human resources"- in the notion of decent work[31].

---

[27]   OIT, *Trabajo decente para la mujer... cit.* p. 14.
[28]   ILO, *Globalising Europe... cit.* p. 28.
[29]   Ditto, p. 27.
[30]   Resolución sobre el Desarrollo de los recursos humanos, adopted at the 88th Meeting (2000) of the International Labour Conference, paras. 18 to 20.
[31]   SOMAVÍA, Juan, *Un trabajo decente para todos en una economía globalizada.... cit.* para 30; ILO, *Proposal for a decent work programme.... cit.* p.p. 38 to 40, 42 and 68.

1. Vocational training as a fundamental right

13.   If decent work is that in which the rights of workers are respected, it seems clear that to achieve it those claims have to be met, in particular the ones that are part of human *rights* or *fundamental rights*.

In that connection, Amartya Sen has pointed out that introduction of the notion of decent work and its promotion as an objective or purpose, underline the importance of working conditions and labour rights at a time when they were perhaps losing influence or might be questioned, in view of widespread unemployment and the consequent inducement to create jobs, whatever their quality. The decent work proposal prevents "unemployment solutions from being used as an excuse for depriving employed persons of reasonable work conditions"[32].

But Sen goes further. In his opinion, the second conceptual characteristic of the ILO initiative in favour of decent work is that it insists on the recognition of rights, (not just compliance with those embodied in current labour legislation, or the introduction of new rights) but acknowledgement of the existence of *fundamental rights that must be recognised although they may not be proclaimed by the legislation, but lie at the root of all decent societies*[33].

14.   Indeed, the right to vocational training has been recognised not only in comparative legislation, in Constitutions and international standards, but is part of that repertory of *human rights* or *fundamental rights*.

In fact, it is beyond argument that nowadays "education and training are a right for all", as categorically stated in paragraph 8 of the Resolution on the development of human resources of the 88th Meeting (2000) of the International Labour Conference.

The right to vocational training has been recognised and institutionalised within the system of fundamental human rights through universal, international, regional or local international standards on human rights, as well as through international labour standards and national Constitutions[34].

---

[32]   SEN, Amartya, *Trabajo y derechos,* en Revista Internacional del Trabajo, Ginebra 2000, vol. 119 N°2, p. 131.

[33]   This concept coincides with the ILO Declaration of Fundamental Labour Principles and Rights, adopted at the International Labour Conference of 1998.

[34]   BARBAGELATA, Héctor-Hugo, (ed.) BARRETTO GHIONE, Hugo and HENDERSON, Humberto, *El derecho a la formación profesional en las normas internacionales,* Cinterfor/OIT, Montevideo 2000, p. 11.

In consequence, the right to vocational training is embodied in the text of many of the most outstanding universal and regional Declarations and Agreements on human rights. *Among others*, the following:

a)   ILO Constitution (Preamble, 1919, and Philadelphia Declaration, 1944);
b)   Universal Declaration of Human Rights (UNO, 1948);
c)   American Declaration of Human Rights and duties (OAS, 1948):
d)   OAS Charter (1948, modified several times since 1967):
e)   European Social Charter (Council of Europe, 1961):
f)   International Pact on Economic, Social and Cultural Rights (UNO, 1966):
g)   Convention of the Americas on Human Rights (OAS, 1978);
h)   Protocol to the Convention of the Americas on Human Rights, or "San Salvador Protocol" (OAS, 1988);
i)   Community Charter of Fundamental Rights of Workers (European Union, 1989);
j)   Social and Labour Declaration of the Mercosur (1998);
k)   Charter of Fundamental Rights of the European Union (2000);
l)   European Union Treaty (latest version: Niza Treaty, 2001).

Likewise, the Constitutions of many countries include the right to training in the repertory of fundamental rights: among others, those of Germany, Argentina, Bolivia, Brazil, Chile, Colombia, Costa Rica, Ecuador, El Salvador, Spain, Guatemala, Honduras, Italy, Mexico, Nicaragua, Panama, Paraguay, Peru, Portugal, Uruguay and Venezuela[35] .

Vocational training has therefore been accepted as a fundamental human right in the main international Agreements and Declarations, and in the Constitutions of a considerable number of countries of the Americas and Europe[36] and is then a principle that decent work has to abide by.

15.   But besides being a basic human right -which is by itself sufficient reason to maintain that a job that does not provide training opportunities cannot be considered decent- vocational training has close links with other fundamental labour rights, and may condition the effectiveness of some of them.

In effect, as we shall see below, the very *right to work* is increasingly dependent on vocational training. The same can be said about the *right to proper working conditions* and to *fair remuneration*. To a great extent, the *right to non-discrimination in employment* is more likely to be attained by adequately trained workers. Voca-

---

[35]   Ditto, pp. 35-36 and 161 and ff. pp.
[36]   Dito, p. 43.

tional training also has close ties with *social dialogue* and with *collective bargaining.*

In other words, *vocational training is a fundamental human right and must be considered as such, along with other rights that have to be respected in decent work; but at the same time it is an instrument that facilitates and sometimes conditions the attainment of other rights that are also part and parcel of decent work.*

16.   On the other hand, the right to vocational training does not only contribute to the shaping of decent work -as we have just explained- but it is educationally a formative element in people's lives, an instrument for the enrichment, self-fulfilment and development of individuals, and through them, of society at large. In the world of labour vocational training -just as education in the global society- is a prerequisite for citizenship, the enjoyment of rights and self fulfilment[37].

This higher -truly superior- dimension of training is expressed in paragraph 4 of article 1 of C 142 Human Resources Development Convention (1975), which states that vocational training and guidance policies and programmes "shall be designed to improve the ability of the individual to understand and, individually or collectively, to influence the working and social enviroment". It has in fact been highlighted that Convention 142 sets forth the *anthropocentric nature* of vocational training, insofar as it proclaims the right of workers to promote their personal development[38].

So that vocational training is not only an integral part of the concept of decent work, but it surrounds it, helping to form an envelope that makes it viable. There will be no decent work without democracy, social justice and citizenship. And there will be none of those without education, vocational training included.

2. Vocational training as an economic instrument

17.   But vocational training is not just a right of workers. It is also an important economic instrument which nurtures active employment policies and the strategies of productivity and competitiveness of enterprises. In that perspective, training is a matter of interest for governments and employers.

---

[37]   In Law, a person is the subject of rights, the holder of rights, he who knows them and can exercise them.
[38]   GARMENDIA ARIGÓN, Mario, *Legislación comparada sobre formación profesional. Una visión desde los convenios de la OIT,* Cinterfor/OIT, Montevideo 2000, pp. 20-22.

It is no longer possible to "achieve higher levels of productivity, competitiveness and quality with an approach of limited and confined training"[39]. Globalisation, the easy movement of capitals -both financial and fixed assets- and technological progress have increasingly turned qualified manpower into a crucial comparative edge[40]. At the same time, as a result of technological progress, the most profitable and enduring kind of competitiveness is achieved through quality and added value, rather than abatement of costs. It is equally obvious that quality and added value also require trained manpower and full use of all human capital, which includes men and women. For that reason there is a close relationship between adequate personnel management, strengthening of corporate competitiveness and equal treatment and labour opportunity.

In addition, it is quite obvious that the productivity of a properly trained worker will be much higher that that of an unskilled one.

For that reason, the Resolution on development of human resources of 2000 declares in paragraph 11 that "the cost of education and training should be seen as an investment". Shortly before that, the ILO Director General had said at the World Trade Organisation that "the application of judicious social policies, with investment in the development of human resources, brings along great benefits, not only social but also economic benefits"[41].

In the particular case of underdeveloped countries, the competitive advantage of having qualified manpower also depends on the countries' capacity to retain the persons they have trained and give them adequate employment in productive activities. Otherwise, the effort made will be useless and frustrating, producing enlightened unemployment, underemployment and emigration. We find here another strong link with decent work. It is necessary to train, but for that investment to be economically profitable, decent jobs must be provided.

18.   Apart from that, vocational training is an important employability factor. Although it does not by itself generate jobs, it greatly helps individuals to compete for available work posts, or to keep whatever employment they have[42]. In that respect, advantages are shared by workers and employers. The latter will have workers with initiative, multifunctional or that way inclined, with an active and competi-

---

[39]   OIT, *Trabajo decente y protección para todos....cit.* p. 38.
[40]   REICH, Robert, *El trabajo de las naciones,* spanish translation, Buenos Aires 1993, pp. 13, 18, 83-84, 139, and 256 to 259.
[41]   SOMAVÍA, Juan, *Un trabajo decente para todos... cit.*
[42]   Cf. paras. 3 and 9 of *Resolución de 2000 sobre Desarrollo de recursos humanos* and ERMIDA URIARTE, Oscar and ROSENBAUM RÍMOLO, Jorge, *Formación profesional en la negociación colectiva,* Cinterfor/OIT. Montevideo 1998, pp. 13-14.

tive attitude; by the same token employees will be able to adapt to change and in a better position to keep their jobs.

Training is therefore a necessary part of all employment policies aiming at employability in a decent job. The higher a worker's qualifications, the greater his employability in a decent job. From this angle, vocational training also promotes the attainment of the decent work goal.

It also works the other way round. Whilst training has a positive effect on decent work, the latter for its part fosters improved training. In effect, skills and abilities are developed to a great extent at work, for which reason decent work provides an adequate environment for training, further training and updating. In that connection ongoing or lifelong training has a leading role. Consequently, in the same manner as training is a prerequisite for decent work, decent work ensures lifelong education. At this point new rights come on the scene -once again- that make training at work viable: they are, specially, time off for attending courses and children's care facilities.

A two way dialectic relationship exists between vocational training and decent work. On the one hand, training is a precondition and constituent of decent work, and on the other, decent work provides an adequate environment for implementing certain kinds of training that are increasingly necessary and important, as we shall see in a moment.

19.   The fundamental incidence of knowledge on development is nowadays an accepted fact. Economies are no longer based only on the accumulation of capital and labour forces; knowledge and information are also increasingly needed. Research brings forth technological and productive innovations. Knowledge has come to be the foundation of man's work and one more factor in production. We nowadays talk about the advent of a *society of knowledge*, in which access to know-how and information is just as important as access to capital was in the industrial society. Consequently, education plays an ever more significant role.

Simultaneously, technological development and in particular the growth of information science, have brought about other important changes in economics and labour. The latest ILO Report on Employment in the World[43] recalls that the technology of communications and information (TCI) could imply one of the greatest economic and social risks faced by our societies.

---

[43]   OIT, *El empleo en el mundo, 2001. La vida en el trabajo y en la economía de la información*, Ginebra 2001.

Therefore, the need to invest in training is becoming more pressing, and if lifelong education already was a prerequisite for employability, it is even more so in the digital age. For new jobs in TCI to be decent more training is needed, in particular more ongoing training[44].

3. Decent Work, vocational training and the ILO strategic objectives

20.   As already indicated, the ILO has been identifying its strategic objectives with some of the components of decent work. It seems clear so far that training is a prerequisite and component of decent work, but all the same it might be useful to point out briefly some special and additional links training has with the ILO objectives.

We have already dwelt on the very close ties between training and the fundamental rights of man, that indeed make of training one more of those rights. We could add here that, as indicated before, *equality in non-discriminatory treatment,* which is one of the principles of the 1998 Declaration, depends, among other things, on access to education and vocational training. In many relegated or disfavoured groups a training deficit is apparent. Inversely, discrimination is less frequent or extreme among workers who have better quality jobs.

As stated in paragraph 6 of the Resolution on development of human resources, 2000, "education and training of high quality are major instruments to improve overall socio-economic conditions, and to prevent and combat social exclusion and discrimination, particulary in employment. In order to be effective they must cover everyone, including disadvantaged groups. Therefore, they must be carefully targeted at women and persons with special needs...".

Regarding specially the gender matter, it has been said that the segregation of women has been determined, or to a great extent promoted by shortcomings in vocational training, both initial training and ongoing learning[45]. In some concrete cases it has been shown that the access to training is irregular and a source of inequity, as those best trained are the ones who demand -and get- further training. Although women's participation in training has been growing steadily, it is still insufficient, usually concentrating at the lower occupational levels or in concrete

[44]   Cf. also ILO, *Globalising Europe.... cit.* p. 27
[45]   OIT, *Trabajo decente para la mujer. Una propuesta de la OIT... cit.* p. 14.

activities that are too specific[46]. Moreover, the recent *digital divide* that we mentioned before compounds gender difficulties. For instance, it has been shown that typical users of the Internet in the world are *male*, under 35, with a college education and high income, English speaking and city dwellers[47].

From the above we may conclude that promoting gender equality at work can be equated with training action focusing on women's employability, so that they also may have access to decent work.[48]. Vocational training can indeed contribute to upgrade the educational opportunities of both men and women, taking into account their different needs and removing the social factors that contribute to women's discrimination at work. For example, the role of education -including vocational training- is essential for giving new value to female tasks in the care of children and elderly persons, and for promoting effective sharing of family responsibilities.

21. We need not insist on the role of training in the promotion of employment, particularly good quality employment, and employability. We may, however, comment on training as an instrument for *social protection*.

The introduction of social protection as an objective of social policies and as a juridical principle can be considered one of the achievements of humanity in the 20th Century. All persons are thereby afforded a minimum level of security *vis-à-vis* the so-called social risks or contingencies, such as sickness, accidents, old age, unemployment or exclusion. Social protection, which includes social security and goes beyond it, consists of the collective intervention of society in order to guard its citizens against various hazards and vulnerabilities, to maintain their welfare and strengthen their capacity to face such risks. Training is an essential element in this concept of social protection, insofar as it must foresee the rehabilitation of workers affected by cutbacks in personnel, offering retraining and unemployment insurance to those that have been laid off[49].

---

[46] VALENZUELA, María E., *Calidad de empleo de las mujeres en el Cono Sur*, mimeographed paper submitted to the international seminar on "Diálogo Social, Tripartismo e Igualdad de Oportunidades en el Mercosur", Santiago, Chile, 2000.

[47] SILVEIRA, Sara, *Políticas públicas de equidad de género en el trabajo en los países del Cono Sur* www.cinterfor.org.uy. See also, by the same author and at the same site, *La política formativa con dimensión de género: avances y desafíos para el nuevo siglo*, presentation submitted to the Primer Seminario Latinoamericano sobre Género y formación profesional, Panama, 2000.

[48] Another relevant matter is whether decent work is the same for men and women, although this is not the place to discuss it.

[49] Report of the UN Secretary General, *El mejoramiento de la protección social y la reducción de la vulnerabilidad en el actual proceso de mundialización*, Comisión de Desarrollo Social, 39th period of sessions, 13-23 February 2001, cit. by BARRETTO GHIONE, Hugo, *Diálogo social y formación...cit.* p. 8.

Important here are training modalities connected with social hazards, particularly unemployment: *training and retraining of unemployed workers; continuous training,* the retraining of *adults;* and the training of *young people* can be mentioned as examples[50].

22.   *Social dialogue,* the fourth ILO strategic objective and also a component of decent work, has in vocational training an appropriate meeting ground where the interests of the different players come together. In effect, the *dual nature* of vocational training (a right of workers on the one hand, a corporate instrument on the other) makes it adequate for a dialogue about traditional bargaining points, that in times of adjustment policies and keen business competition tends to turn sour and difficult.

The Resolution on development of human resources, quoted here several times, devotes several long and very apt paragraphs to social dialogue and vocational training.

Among other provisions, Paragraph 18 states that "trade unions and employers' associations (...) also contribute to training by managing their own training institutions and providing education for their members", and thereupon adds that "collective bargaining can set appropriate conditions for the organisation and implementation of training". Paragraph 19 points out that "the social partners should strengthen social dialogue on training, share responsibility in formulating education and training policies, and engage in partnerships with each other or with governments for investing in planning and implementing training". It goes on "governments should establish a framework for effective social dialogue and partnerships in training and employment".

Then, paragraph 20 finds that "the scope and effectiveness of social dialogue and partenerships in training is currently limited by the capacity and resources of actors", which leads on to the ILO strategic objective of buttressing the social actors in order to promote dialogue.

In what seems to be a significant conclusion, paragraph 20 of the Resolution ends up by saying that, "being a tripartite organisation, the ILO should lead international co-operation to build up capacities for social dialogue and partnership building in training". It finally adds that "additional efforts would have to be made for the benefit of developing countries"

---

[50]   See *supra.* para 12.

26

Pursuant to this mandate, in co-operation with other ILO offices, departments and programmes, Cinterfor/ILO has promoted the implementation of a number of studies on the subject, and has started publication of a Series on "Contributions to Social Dialogue and Training"[51]

23.   Based on the above, the present study will be divided into four parts, each one of which will consider the role of vocational training in the attainment of the ILO strategic objectives which, in turn, have been deemed components of the concept and objective of decent work.

---

[51]   The following titles have already been issued: ROSENBAUM RÍMOLO, Jorge, *Negociación colectiva sobre formación en el Mercosur,* Montevideo 2000; CAPPELLETTI, Beatriz and others, *Actores sociales y formación en Argentina,* Montevideo 2000: DIEESE, *Diálogo social sobre formaçao no Brasil,* Montevideo 2000; REYNOSO CASTILLO, Carlos, *Diálogo social sobre formación en México,* Montevideo, 2000; CÉSPEDES, Roberto, *Diálogo social sobre formación en Paraguay,* Montevideo, 2001; and ROSENBAUM RÍMOLO, Jorge, *Diálogo social sobre formación en Uruguay,* Montevideo, 2001; and BARRETTO GHIONE, Hugo, *Diálogo social y formación: una perspectiva desde los países del Mercosur y México,* Montevideo 2001.

II
VOCATIONAL TRAINING
AND ITS LINKS WITH EQUAL OPPORTUNITY
AND OTHER FUNDAMENTAL RIGHTS

The right to vocational training

24.   We have already pointed out that nowadays the right to vocational training has been recognised as a human right by most Declarations and Pacts on fundamental rights and by various national constitutions[52] . We need not therefore reiterate it, although we may add that the legislation of various countries is increasingly demarcating and regulating the nature and scope of that right. We may add that the right to training is currently part of the labour law or the doctrinal interpretation thereof in a growing number of countries.

That is also reflected in the jurisdiction of labour administration, as Ministries of Labour have shouldered training responsibilities, developing specialised bodies for that purpose and sometimes incorporating such attributions to their name. That has taken place, for instance, in Argentina. ("Ministry of Labour, Employment, and Human Resources' Training") and in France ("Ministry of Employment and Training").

25.   On the other hand, recognition of the workers' subjective right to vocational training necessitates its counterpart: workers would be obliged to do their utmost, in good faith, to take advantage of the training offered to them. In Law this is called an *obligation of means* (not *ends*): workers would not have to "guarantee" the attainment of the skills levels aimed at by the training, but they would have to make a reasonable effort to profit by it.

26.   As already indicated, the mere fact of its being a fundamental right, makes vocational training a component of decent work, as no work could be qualified as such if did not embody compliance with human rights. But besides that, as also pointed out, the right to vocational training is a precondition for other labour entitle-

[52]   See above, para. 13.

ments of a fundamental nature, as the right to work itself, to a fair, equitable and sufficient remuneration, and others of the same order, apart from those included in the 1998 ILO Declaration.

The right to vocational training and its links with other fundamental rights

27.   Even in an abridged formulation, a decent job is at least sufficient in quantity and *quality*[53], which presupposes the effectiveness of certain rights. A technical paper prepared by the ILO Pilot Programme on Decent Work[54] lists the following rights to be complied with for a job or occupation to qualify as decent:

- the right to work or employment, i.e. access to employment;
- the right to fair working conditions;
- the right ro equal and sufficient wages;
- the right to secure work, i.e. ensuring safety and hygiene;
- the right to an enduring job, as protection against unemployment;
- the right to social protection, including social security;
- the right to vocational training;
- the right of taking part in decisions that may affect one;
- and, of course, the other principles and rights enshrined in the 1998 ILO Declaration, like for instance union freedom, collective bargaining and non-discrimination.

Inclusion in this list of the right to training as one of the rights that form part of decent work, ratifies the dual role of vocational training: on the one hand it is one of the elements that make up decent work, and on the other, it is also a precondition for the exertion of other rights that make it up, and therefore a prerequisite for the decency of a job.

28.   For instance, it is quite evident that the *right to work* itself is increasingly dependent on appropriate training. We have already said, and we shall insist on this later, that vocational training is a requirement for employability. Furthermore, the skills or competencies of workers, which traditionally were only considered when they were engaged for a job, in the present-day framework of flexible production and constant technological change, are the object of scrutiny all along their labour performance. They are a requirement for adaptability to change, for "multifunctionality", and in this way for *job permanence*. So, the right to training is

---

[53]   BARRETTO GHIONE, Hugo, *Concepto y dimensiones del trabajo decente: entre la protección social básica y la participación de los trabajadores en la empresa* (unpublished, para. 36).

[54]   EGGER, Philippe, and SENGENBERGER Werner, op. cit. par. 1.

not only an employment access requirement, but also for *job permanance and protection.*

29.   Likewise, the competencies that workers may have acquired through training, will undoubtedly have an effect on their *remuneration*, making *fair and sufficient pay* more of a reality. Openings for *promotion and a labour career* will also increase, just as, for example, Mexico's Federal Labour Law foresees. In this respect, continuous or life long training is essential.

30.   The right to training is also closely related to *working conditions.* It seems quite obvious that the higher the skills and competencies workers have, the greater will be their possibilities of getting better working conditions, time off and an adequate labour environment. On the other hand, accomplishment of the right to training, that -as we have repeatedly declared, is in itself a fundamental right and consequently an end in itself- requires the enforcement of some specific rights and working conditions such as, for instance, time off for training and day care centres.

It is essential in that connection to mention Convention 140 and Recommendation 148 concerning Paid Educational Leave (1974). A Brazilian rule is also worth mentioning that provides for breaks in the labour contract for training purposes, under union supervision, and grants substituting for wages during training periods.

Including time off for training during the labour relationship is a matter of great importance for the future, as it ties the reduction of working hours with the ongoing training that is essential for job conservation and the increase of productivity. The issue is in this way related to a trend that can be discerned in the future, namely, the transformation of current labour relations into alternative labour and training covenants[55] .

31.   The development of training also encourages workers' *motivation and involvement.* At the same time, it seems obvious that better trained workers are likely to be more aware of their rights and obligations, i.e. more responsible workers, capable of participation. Under such circumstances, *participation* by workers in decision-making that may concern them will occur in more favourable conditions if they are able professionals.

We might conclude this section quoting a formulation of recent doctrine, whereby the attainment of decent work presupposes two levels of action in the

[55]   SUPIOT, Alain (Co-ord.), *Trabajo y Empleo,* Spanish translation, Valencia 1999, and SUPIOT Alain, *Transformaciones del trabajo y derecho laboral en Europa,* en Revista Internacional del Trabajo, Ginebra 1999, vol. 119 N°1, p. 35 and following pp.

area of labour rights. *A first level* calls for the *protection of basic labour rights*, not just those provided for in the ILO Declaration of 1998, but also those enshrined as human rights in international Pacts and Declarations, as well as in national Constitutions. *A second level* implies the *promotion of autonomy and participation*[56], which are instruments for advancing the civic education of workers. Vocational training is a human right to be protected, and a prerequisite for the advancement of workers' participation and autonomy.

Vocational training as an instrument for equal opportunity

32.   Focusing now on the role of vocational training in the attainment of the principles and rights expressly reflected in the ILO Declaration of 1998, we can recall that they are the recognition and promotion of trade union freedom and collective bargaining, banishment of forced labour, child labour and discrimination regarding employment and work. All these tenets are an essential, we could say *minimal,* part of decent work. And vocational training contributes, sometimes crucially, to their attainment, in particular regarding the banning of forced labour, child labour and discrimination.

33.   In effect, the abolition of forced labour depends on a number of factors, *one of which is* no doubt, access to certain levels of elementary education and vocational training, without which the free choice of work would be impossible in certain economic, political and juridical contexts.

34.   Something similar could be said regarding the eradication of child labour, wherein restrictive and repressive action must go hand in hand with other long-term measures ensuring the permanence of deterrence. Among them, basic education is essential, as well as training, to a certain degree, as foreseen in the first report of the ILO Director General on decent work, which underlines that it is not enough to prevent children from working. It is also necessary to give them "opportunities for education" and "appropriate educational alternatives"[57].

35.   It is also clear that proscribing labour discrimination requires the promotion of equality, especially in those areas that are more exposed to discrimination. Disabled persons, youngsters and women are three of the groups that most frequently undergo employment difficulties, the first two of them in particular regarding access to work.

---

[56]   BARRETTO GHIONE, Hugo, Concepto y dimensiones del trabajo decente..., cit. para. 26 and following paras.

[57]   OIT, *Trabajo decente,* cit, p.19.

36.   In connection with physically or mentally 'challenged' people, a provision of the Mercosur Social and Labour Declaration may be mentioned which, apart from including the right to vocational training among the fundamental entitlements of the Region, makes special reference to the training of the disabled. After proclaiming that "persons with physical or mental disabilities shall be treated in a dignified, non-discriminatory manner, favouring their social and labour inclusion", it provides in Article 2 that "member States undertake to adopt effective measures, especially regarding their education, training, retraining and vocational guidance..." etc.

37.   Needless to say, young people are another group with difficulties of access to employment. The role of vocational training is of fundamental importance in mitigating such difficulties. In the last decade, despite progress made in the field of education, the labour market has not yet been able to generate a flow of good enough jobs for the new-coming population. Employment dynamics are based on the growth of low-productivity sectors, mainly independent workers and micro-enterprises. Most young men and women, particularly those in more vulnerable situation due to the low socio-ecnomic level of their homes and their traditional educational shortcomings, tend to find jobs in low productivity sectors. Those occupations are usually precarious, self employed, sometimes unremunerated.

38.   It can also be noted, in general, that the links between the labour market and the behaviour of the economy have changed. When economies go into recession, there is a shrinking of employment offer and, consequently, unemployment tends to grow. Longer recessive periods give rise to lasting unemployment situations that are difficult to redress even when growth picks up. This is due mainly to two factors: firstly, because those affected by long unemployment (one year or more) find it very difficult to get a job again, even when the new context is more favourable; secondly, because many people give up looking for a job during the recession, but resume their search when the economic situation improves; this brings about an increase of the labour supply simultaneously with the increased demand, which tends to maintain unemployed levels unaltered. Young job seekers are particularly hit by this type of relation between the economic cycle and employment. In periods of growth they tend to be the last to engage, and in periods of recession they are the first to jettison. Youth employment goes along with the economic cycle, but when labour markets shrink the young are affected more than other groups. In recessive periods, youth unemployment rates swell much more than adult unemployment, even as both are dependent on overall activity.

39.   Nevertheless, the behaviour of unemployment, as well as that of under-employment, informality and precarious work varies according to the internal diversity of the young population. If just the fact of being young means a greater probability of being affected by these problems, that probability is often compounded by other

factors such as sex, race or social and economic background. Vocational training then appears as a positive tool for countering existing inter-generation inequalities. But through focalised strategies it can also contribute to solve complex exclusion situations, as those resulting from a combination of characteristics that create inequity of access to decent work. In chapter III of this paper we go further in diagnosing the situation of the young vis-à-vis employment and vocational training, and in experiences and programmes specifically intended for young people in Latin America and the Caribbean.

40.   The racial factor cannot be omitted among those causing discrimination at work, under certain circumstances. An analysis of training careers in racial minorities and the way in which modifying such careers might improve and even out their labour possibilities is not approached here, in view of the specific nature of this document. The issue merits special consideration, and we take due note of it.

41.   It is quite evident that the promotion of gender equality in access to work and labour promotion is one of the most important aspects, one that has generated a multiplicity of activities and studies. The 1999 Report of the ILO Director General already declared that " to apply an integrated policy regarding equality between the sexes", it would be necessary to develop "adequate standards concerning training and personnel, that may favour the occupational advancement of women".

42.   At the beginning of the 21st Century it is unquestionable that sustainable economic and social development must focus on persons, and consequently ensure - both in public and private spheres- that women should benefit unrestrictedly from all rights and enjoy full participation on the same footing as men. In spite of all this, reality repeatedly shows how far we are from full compliance with that objective. To varying degrees and with different nuances according to country, social, cultural and economic conditions, restrictions, segmentations and demands are imposed on women that curb their basic human rights and their civic entitlements and, in a particularly blunt manner, their access to employment and their personal and career development. This points to the need of persistent efforts to overcome the situation.

43.   In Latin America, the item *"gender equity"* has only recently been included in the agenda of public policies dealing with problems of employment, vocational and technical training, and it has been approached in many different and fragmentary ways. The issue emerged owing to the notorious increase of female participation in education and in the economically active population, to the efforts and legitimacy of the women's movement in the last two decades, and the type and quality of the knowledge that has been accumulated concerning gender relations. Greater emphasis on it both in international co-operation programmes and national policies has also derived from an increasing international consensus about the need

for greater equity and sustainability in development processes, and current concerns about threats to quality of life and the environment. This consensus has led to a stronger commitment to the struggle against poverty and gender inequality. Fear for the endangered quality of our lives is also promoting a revaluation of participation and collective organisations. The weight that *gender equity* has acquired in the last twenty years rests on the efforts and lessons learned in a great number of programmes that endeavoured to find an answer to women's problems and needs, and to a recognition of their rights and contributions to development.

44.   The Latin American vocational training system has devised various approaches and implemented programmes and activities within the framework and conditions of global and regional trends regarding our countries' economic and social development. It has also been influenced by social ideas concerning female and male roles. This meant initially remedial and assistance activities of literacy support, that for women emphasised family planning, health care and training in manual tasks, home economics, etc. As from the 1970s, growing poverty and female unemployment shifted attention towards productive activities and the need for women to generate their own income. There was a boom of training in support of self-employment and micro-enterprises, which to a great extent overlooked the human and economic viability and sustainability of such undertakings. In the 1980s, specific vocational and technical education programmes for women were started. In the late 1980s stress was laid on women's participation in non-traditional areas, in combination with micro-enterprise activities, in order to improve their access to better remunerated jobs. This was a changeover from an approach that was based specially on the needs of poor women, taking them as passive beneficiaries of development policies, towards a human rights approach that recognised women as active participants entitled to their rights on an equal footing with men. From the point of view of training policies, there was an effort to adapt to the new context, but it also showed that, unless clear-cut specific measures were taken, exclusion and discrimination patterns emerged again. The positive side is that it enabled us to learn how to use training to counteract such tendencies.

45.   A clear example of this complex interaction is occupational segmentation by gender. This segmentation is governed by differential social attributions of roles, places and values by sex, which is first learnt at home, reaffirmed in school and subsequently crystallised in occupational options. For instance, the internalisation of stereotypes and preconceptions about women's inability to perform technical jobs, turns into inner repression mechanisms that mould our wishes, expectations and motivations in such a way that some occupational options seem "*naturally oriented*". Choices determined by rigid standards are then considered to be the result of free will. Training systems also have their own internal barriers, such as an absence or shortage of occupational information or guidance with a gender slant; the persistence of a sexist language in the dissemination of training offers

and teaching aids, as well as in curricula, methodological and teaching practices. There is also a lack of flexibility in course organisation; women's needs are not foreseen in training infrastructures, and they have little participation in upper management and technical teaching jobs. Other factors are added, such as scarce relevance for females of the training supplied; non-existence of placement services or coaching to look for a job, which mainly affects women as they require special support to shed existing prejudices and break into new areas of activity, with better possibilities for them. The result of all this is a double segmentation, by levels and occupations, which despite all efforts still characterises female participation in vocational training in the Region. This division into compartments is subsequently confirmed and reinforced in the labour market.

46.   The conviction that to overcome this kind of interplay programmes and strategies were required to deal with the problem of women's participation in an overall manner, and that vocational training policies should be linked to their context in a dual way, led in the early 1990s to a prioritisation of the concept of *equity,* and of *gender equity* in particular. The context of reality conditions and determines training activities, and at the same time promotes them and poses challenges to them. Training policies should be relevant and in keeping with the requirements of social and economic development. They also can and should become an instrument to combat the different forms of social exclusion and inequality that the development model itself nurtures. In declaring that "gender equity is a mater of human rights and social justice, and a requirement for economic development", the ILO assumes a proactive role in his connection. A qualitative leap forward was made in Latin American training with the *Programa de Promoción de la Participación de la Mujer en la Formación Técnica y Profesional (Programme for Promoting Women's Participation in Vocational and Technical Training)* jointly carried out by the former Regional Consultant Service for Working Women, of the Turin International Training Centre, and Cinterfor/ILO. Fifteen vocational training institutes took part in this project, showing their interest and capacity for action in this field.[58] This programme achieved a remarkable synergy in the dissemination and exchange of methodologies and strategies, and in working out an overall proposal as to how to act from training policies to improve gender equity in employment and education, and in building support and co-operation networks. It became a main landmark in gender themes, and served as conceptual and methodological source for the design and implementation of training policies with a gender slant. Chapter III of this Document delves deeper into various experiences that are being implemented in the Region in this field.

---

[58]   CONET (Argentina), SENAI and SENAC (Brazil), SENA (Colombia), INA (Costa Rica), INACAP (Chile), SECAP (Ecuador), DGCC and ICIC (Mexico), INATEC (Nicaragua), SENATI (Peru), INFOTEP (Dominican Republic), Instituto ORT and CETP/UTU (Uruguay) and INCE (Venezuela).

III
VOCATIONAL TRAINING
AND EMPLOYMENT PROMOTION

47.   Offering women and men more opportunities of obtaining a decorous job and income is one of the ILO strategic objectives for the 2002-2003 biennium. Decent work, support to employment policies, investment in the development of theoretical and practical knowledge, employability and the creation of jobs, are the lines of action the Organisation intends to follow to reach this goal. There is clearly a close link between vocational training and investment in knowledge and the promotion of employability. Equally important is the contribution training can make in the framework of active labour market policies and strategies for raising productivity and competitiveness. This Chapter tries to go deeper into the nature of that contribution, both in the conceptual plane and concerning regional experiences in that respect.

Vocational training, employment and employability

48.   Foremost among the many ways in which vocational training is often called upon to play a role, are strategies intended to expand the employment offered and improve its quality. Consequently, over and above the many variants of what are known as "active employment policies", vocational training should always appear as a strategic, if not a fundamental, component.

49.   The close connection of training to such themes is undeniable and stems from its original and cardinal mission: preparing persons for the world of labour. Based on that mission, vocational training aims at developing abilities to perform efficiently in productive organisations, either of goods or services. There is then, at least in theory, a 'matching up' of what a job requires in terms of knowledge, abilities and skills and those that vocational training delivers or passes on.

50.   As an effect of this 'matching up' process, an answer has been sought in vocational training to the problem of unemployment, which is not only expanding but also acquiring structural and permanent characteristics. However, in this search the fact is often overlooked that training can only directly adapt its contents and

37

methods to a productive, technological and labour reality, and in no way act as a genuine source of employment generation.

51. Unemployment analysts frequently try to get down to its roots. They generally reach the conclusion that unemployment is mainly due to structural causes, i.e. causes connected with the scant capacity of the economy as a whole to create jobs for reasons such as absence of investment (public or private), problems of competitiveness of enterprises and economic sectors, technological recycling and updating, etc. The other two causes usually adduced to explain (in part) unemployment, are the inefficiency or non-existence of communication and information channels to co-ordinate manpower supply and demand, or a mismatch of the competencies required by companies and the labour market in general, and those offered by the educational system and vocational training in particular.

52. As these two last causes only in part explain unemployment, it is quite obvious that measures to correct them will not solve the overall problem. Nevertheless, the fact that such measures have a potentially secondary role does not necessarily mean that they are futile. Quite the contrary: although its effects may be limited, action in those areas is essential. To stress this concept, we may recall that it is precisely there that the contribution both of training and vocational guidance can be more effective and visible.

53. The need for adequate co-ordination between training and vocational guidance services was already stated in Convention142 concerning Vocational Guidance and Vocational Training in the Development of Human Resources, as far back as 1975. Article 1, Item 1 establishes that "Each Member shall adopt and develop comprehensive and co-ordinated policies and programmes of vocational guidance and vocational training, closely linked with employment, in particular through public employment services". This concept has been picked up again recently in the Resolution on development of human resources at the 88th Meeting of the International Labour Conference, in June 2000. It reads there that "Besides education and training, vocational guidance and placement services (careers development services) that include education and careers' counselling, counselling on employment and information on education, training and the labour market, are all measures that play an essential role in the development of human resources" (Item 8, second paragraph).

54. In line with the above, but based mainly on a diagnosis of their own situation, most countries of the Region have adopted co-ordination strategies between their training, occupational guidance and placement services.

55. On the other hand, the search for an adequate 'fit' or equivalence between the skills structure offered and the present or emerging requirements of enter-

prises and the labour market in general, is one of the most systematic and basic strivings of vocational training in Latin America and the Caribbean. The effort is made regarding job profiles in demand but also technological upgrading, the organisation and management of production and labour, and the attention of more numerous and diverse users needing training services.

56.   This is taking place both in vocational training institutions and in Ministries of Labour and Education. Efforts are mainly aimed at improving what nowadays is known as 'employability', a characteristic that has a conceptual and practical relationship with employment. It embodies all the qualifications, knowledge and competences that may improve the capacity of workers to improve their performance and adapt to change, get another job when they wish to do so or when they are laid off, and to integrate more easily into the labour market at different stages of their life. This means that investing in improving the employability of people may have a positive effect on curbing the type of unemployment caused by a scarcity of properly trained candidates for already existing job openings. But it also can have a welcome effect in another sense: if opportunities for accessing training are equitable -and the achievement of higher levels of employability is consequently just as fair- we may predict that opportunities of access to employment will also be equitable, even when employment has ceased to expand or is receding.

57.   In the critical situation of high unemployment affecting large numbers of workers in most countries of the Region, there is a specially serious problem, that of persons that remain unemployed for a long time. Unemployment lasting more than one year brings to those who suffer it consequences that go beyond the lack of a regular income. Those men and women workers are not only prevented from keeping abreast with knowledge, but also lose their connections -what has been called their 'social capital'- which excludes them even further from the labour market. In this respect, vocational training can be a tool to counteract, at least in part, the harmful effects of long standing unemployment, by promoting greater job turnover and guarding against the risks of obsolescence.

58.   It results from the above that vocational training is not a sufficient precondition to deal with the problem of unemployment, but it is absolutely necessary. In general terms, vocational training is one of the tools that, in combination with others, can help to build up a platform from which unemployment can be combated.

59.   Why emphasise employability? What is the meaning of 'training for employability' in the current context? It is justified by a twofold conviction: on the one hand that -as already indicated- employment is no longer generated massively in this current context. It has to be produced through entrepreneurial capacity and co-operation strategies. Job conservation requires a capacity for constant adaptation and learning, in order to deal with changes in contents and modes, in the way

things are done. Hence the prioritisation of employability. On the other hand, it is based on the fact that employability is also related to processes occurring at various levels (structural, normative and cultural levels). For example, productive, organisational and gender relations paradigms impinge upon labour demand and on people's social and educational position, so that certain groups in society have greater difficulties for becoming integrated and achieving labour development.

60.   The impact that new information and communication technologies (ICT) are producing in the competitiveness and productivity strategies of countries, regions, sectors and enterprises and its involvement for the employability of persons, deserves a special mention. These technologies have a powerful effect on production costs, making possible the coexistence of high levels of growth with low inflation. It is gradually being noticed that the electronic markets can be more transparent than the traditional ones, with lower costs of transaction and with the result of substantial changes in the established price relations. In relation to this matter, there is evidence that electronic markets can result a 15% cheaper for consumers. In consequence, the ICT sector is the one that registers the more rapid increment in the industrialised countries. The "digital divide" between these countries and those of other regions like Latin America and the Caribbean, constitutes a first order challenge, due to its effects on competitiveness and productivity issues, challenge that moves in all its magnitude to institutions, systems and vocational training policies. In this last sense the ICT are posing requirements not only in terms of formative contents, but also on the modalities and learning-teaching methodologies. It is imperative to endow male and female workers with the knowledge and necessary tools for the control and use of these technologies, since day after day this is more transformed into a key component of their employability. It also corresponds to vocational training to undertake the challenge of making the access to necessary competencies for the use of ICT as universal and even-handed as possible, in such a way that the existing digital divide on a global scale is not reproduced in national societies. Additionally, ICT possess a feature of being at the same time a goal in itself and a means for achieving other objectives: its adaptation and control by workers is an objective itself, but at the same time they offer greater and innovative alternatives for developing a more flexible training offer and covering geographical areas and groups that today do not have access to the formative services.

61.   Employability is also related with personal aspects. Individuals with an equal social background and formative resources can interpret a particular situation in different ways. Hence, it is possible that they assume an active or passive role in relation with their labour history and, in consequence, may produce different mobilisation of their available resources. In thinking employability from a training perspective, it is necessary to take into account the cultural and personal aspects, since it is from the last mentioned that people can have a more direct control, not

40

only regarding employment, but also over their personal development and the social integration.

62.   For that reason, under current circumstances training for employability means:

- building up people's capacity to improve their possibilities of access to labour by developing key competencies that may guard against obsolescence an enable men and women to remain active and productive along life, not necessarily in the same work post or activity;
- training persons for a permanent and complex learning process that implies: learning to learn, learning to be and learning to do;
- helping persons to identify the internal and external obstacles hindering them in the attainment of their objectives, and to value their own abilities and know-how, as well as the demands and competencies of the world of labour. This includes information and guidance on the educational and labour markets displaying all their various alternatives, requirements and possibilities, doing away with stereotypes that class certain jobs as female or male, and making posible the search for and/or generation of employment.

Vocational training in active employment policies

63.   Employment policies have undergone a transformation process in Latin America and the Caribbean that is directly related to the changes that have taken place in the organisation, distribution and characteristics of work in general and of employment in particular.

64.   Formerly, labour market policies were fundamentally aimed at making up for the harmful effects that periods of economic recession had on the economy. Although it was generally felt that in the long run the economy would tend towards sustained growth -and therefore the same would happen to employment- those periods of recession had serious consequences, albeit limited and circumstantial. The expansion and development of social coverage systems like unemployment insurance, combined with emergency employment schemes were the strategies then used. As there was no problem of structural and permanent unemployment, it was thought that such actions and policies were enough to deal with those cyclical issues.

65.   The advent not only of longer recession periods but also -and mainly- of unemployment as a permanent and recalcitrant problem even during growth cycles, made it necessary to reformulate strategies. What are now known as 'active employment policies' are rightly so called to differentiate them explicitly from former policies that have been renamed as 'passive' or 'remedial' policies.

66. Active employment policies are also intended to have a strategic and integrating effect. They are not unilateral measures in a single, specific institutional area but always imply a degree of complexity insofar as they display a number of lines of action aimed at the same objectives. Although they present a great diversity and varying design their main common characteristic is that they try to have an incidence on those factors that reduce or thwart the growth of employment, or those that cause rigidity, mismatch or lack of communication between employment supply and demand. They do not entail the disappearance of traditional mechanisms like unemployment insurance; they serve instead as a complement to systems that have been overwhelmed by the magnitude and seriousness of labour market problems. In other words, they are policies that aim at the root of problems rather than at their ultimate consequences.

67. Together with the implementation of such policies, there is an open debate as to their co-ordination with other areas of public policy, such as economy, technology and education. This is due to the fact that there is increasing recognition of the decisive influence on employment of factors such as exchange rates, interest rates, support of innovation and scientific and technological development, or investments in education with long-term results, through their impact on competitiveness and productivity.

68. The active employment policies that are being enacted share the following features, to a greater or lesser extent:

• They are complex policy mechanisms that tend to include different types of measures, incentives and occasionally subsidies. They increasingly involve various public organisations of different kinds, as well as private and civil society actors, often promoting a decentralisation of activities at different stages.
• They develop instruments for the prospecting or surveillance of labour markets, that try to establish trends in employment creation or reduction, as well as changes in job contents.
• They set up information and occupational guidance services, on the assumption that at least part of the unemployment is due not to structural causes but to inefficient communication between supply and demand.
• They incorporate training as a key element, on the understanding that part of the mismatch between labour supply and demand is caused by a lack of equivalence between the competencies of job seekers and those effectively in demand by employers.
• They also supplement such action with measures to make up for other personal or social shortfalls (remedial training, internships, etc.)

69. Apart from the degree of advancement of these common features in the various countries of the Region, we shall go here in greater detail into the role that

vocational training develops in the framework of active employment policies. In this framework the training component takes on different characteristics according to the target populations of the different programmes and projects. In a schematic way, the following situations may arise:

• *Initial training for first-time job seekers* within the context of youth training and employment programmes. Projects like "**Chile Joven**", **(Chile)**, **"Proyecto Joven"**, **(Argentina)**, the **Subprograma de capacitación de jóvenes** (Occupational Training Sub-programme for the Young) within the **Programa de Capacitación Laboral para Jóvenes y Trabajadores en Empresas, (PROCAL), (Bolivia)**, the **School-Leavers Training Opportunities Programme, (SL-TOP), (Jamaica)**, "**Projoven**", **(Peru)** or "**Projoven**", **(Uruguay)** are all targeted on this population. They usually offer a short training period in various trades (3-4 months) supplemented by occupational guidance and internships providing an initial labour experience.

• *Retraining of workers who are unemployed or risk losing their jobs.* This may range from supplementary courses to complete rehabilitation in fresh skills. In this category the Programa de Becas a trabajadores en seguro de paro (Programme of grants for workers on unemployment pay) of the Ministerio de Trabajo y Seguridad Social, financed by the Fondo de Reconversión Laboral -FRL- (Labour Retraining Fund), in Uruguay, or the programmes implemented in Brazil by various agencies within the framework of PLANFOR, financed by the Fundo de Amparo ao Trabalhador -FAT- (Fund for Workers' Protection), try to look after this type of population, on the assumption that a social and personal investment in training will result in the higher employability of those workers.

• *Training of active, employed workers to face processes of productive reorganisation and restructuring or technological innovation in different enterprises or sectors.* It is in this area that more examples are to be found of co-ordination between vocational training and collective bargaining by branch of activity or individual company, favoured by State machinery. It is also fertile ground for bipartite experiences in training management. An example of this kind of programme, intended for workers in the public sector, is the "**Reconversión laboral de trabajadores de las empresas pública capitalizadas**" ("Occupational retraining of workers in capitalised public enterprises") in **Bolivia**. Similar to it, but in the private sector, are the **Comités Bipartitos de Capacitación por Empresa** (Bipartite Committees for Training by Firms), in Chile, the experiences of the **Fábrica Nacional de Papel -FANAPEL-** (National Pulp & Paper Plant) and the **construction industry in Uruguay**, or some components of the "Integrar" Programme, of the **Confederação Nacional dos Metalúrgicos (CNM) of the Central Única dos Trabalhadores (CUT)**, with financing provided by the FAT, in Brazil.

43

• *Training for owners of micro-enterprises and self employed workers.* This usually fits into broader plans that include technical assistance and courses providing instruction not only in specific trades, but in matters such as access to credit, marketing, co-ordination among enterprises, technological innovation, business management, etc. The importance ascribed to programmes of this type is due to the relatively dynamic behaviour of the target sectors for generating jobs, although usually such employment is precarious. Examples are "**Productores Agrícolas**" of the **Servicio Nacional de Capacitación y Empleo -SENCE-** (National Training and employment Service), in **Chile** and the **Programa de Calidad Integral y Modernización -CIMO- (Mexico).**

• *Training dispensed as a complementary mechanism to facilitate the generation of earnings by vulnerable groups and sectors.* It includes most programmes for the benefit of women heads of households, whose objectives may be raising the level of employability of beneficiaries, the development of productive commercial undertakings or the generation of supplementary income. Examples of such initiatives are the **Programa Piloteando Futuros** co-ordinated by the **Centros de Estudios de la Mujer** (Centre for Women's Studies) and financed by the Inter-American Development Bank in **Argentina**, and the **Programa Mujeres Jefas de Hogar** (Programme for Women Heads of Households) implemented by the **SENCE** jointly with the **Servicio Nacional de la Mujer -(SERNAM)-** in **Chile.**

• *Local skills development.* The **Community Based Training (CBT)** is one of Special programmes conducted by **HEART/NTA** of **Jamaica.** CBT programmes are usually run by NGOs and community-based organisations, as well as occasionally by other autonomous institutions. The content of their training programmes is oriented towards the demand for local skills development and they are, for the most part, attached to projects promoting the establishment of local enterprises. HEART TRUST/NTA plans to diversify the financing of CBT programmes by promoting income-generating measures in the programmes. The **Learning for Earning Activity Programme -LEAP-** is a mixed programme, offering housing, food and health services as well as remedial and basic vocational training to street children. Programmes addressing the needs of special target groups, including LEAP, cater for about 1,000 persons per year. The total enrolment in community-based projects in 1999/00 was 2,770.

The **Skills 2000 Project,** which was launched in co-operation with the World Food Programme in 1995 (WFP-assistance ended in 2000), aims at enabling poor people who have not completed an educational career to make a basic living and improve their educational profile with regard to further training (pre-level 1 courses). By 1998, the Skills 2000 programme had enrolled almost 3000 trainees into 36 discrete projects. However the programme took longer than expected to gain sufficient support from local enterprises and enterprise development projects and thus from a sufficient funding scheme that was supposed to be derived from efficient partnerships with the private sector and strong income generating components in the programme. Enrolment in Skills 2000 projects was 2,093 in 1999/00.

70. The above enumeration does not exhaust all the variety of combinations that exist in the different countries and are the result of simultaneous lines of action. Besides, many programmes are intended for diverse populations and situations, and sometimes include several secondary projects. It is important however, to underline the central role played in all of them by training and skills development. Although many variants may be found among the experiences of the various countries of the Region, these policies share some common traits. First and foremost, they tend to blend a number of social and economic elements; they try to encompass the different dimensions of unemployment and employment issues and lay stress on focalisation, as opposed to the universal policies that were applied before.

71. Among components to be found in this new generation of active labour market policies are the following:

• economic assistance mechanisms for workers who wish to train or retrain. such as grants and scholarships;
• mechanisms to support access to work, either through information and placement services, or the negotiation of internships at firms and enterprises under the legal guise of "apprenticeship contracts";
• mechanisms for financial assistance -mainly credit- to production and service units, or tax exemptions for training and personnel development activities;
• mechanisms for technical assistance and counselling to productive units on aspects such as: planning, accounting, management and development of human resources, technological development and transfer, marketing, strategic alliances, etc.;
• mechanisms to encourage the supply of vocational training, mainly through tenders and bids for the delivery of public programmes.

72. Nevertheless, whatever the specific form of those policies, their backbone is always vocational training and skills development. Concrete types of training offers are generally adapted to the requirements and characteristics of the groups and populations they are intended to serve.

Vocational training in strategies to raise productivity

73. Generally defined, productivity is the relationship between the production obtained by a system or service and the resources used to obtain it. Consequently,

productivity can be described as an efficient use of resources – labour, capital, the land, raw materials, energy, information- for the production of different goods and services. It can also be defined as the relationship between results and the time it takes to get them: the shorter the time, the more productive the system. Although sometimes productivity is linked to the 'pitch' or intesiveness of work, more often than not it means an extra effort or "increment" of work, which generally brings about only a small increase of productivity. It is usually said that the essence for improving productivity is to work more intelligently, not just harder[59].

74.   Although there are different approaches and types of programmes to raise productivity, there is a basic consensus that no new technique or modern plan can be effectively applied for that purpose without well trained and properly instructed personnel at all levels of the national economy[60].

75.   Various studies have shown that there is a positive correlation between education and training, and productivity. Even a basic comparison of the economic performance of the different countries shows that the best results -regarding both productivity levels and rates of economic growth- are obtained in countries where people are better educated.

76.   In a final analysis, technology is an output of education, culture, creativity, motivation and management systems. In the longer perspective, we may envisage productivity as a kind of mindset based on education and culture, that nurtures the capacity to organise things. Education and vocational training may therefore be seen as important means to speed up the upgrading and quality of the labour force. Persons are in the long run the main productive resource, and in consequence, the most important factor to be considered. In turn, they are a factor with unlimited development possibilities.

77.   Globalisation and the rapid evolution of production systems create new opportunities but also new problems for employment. Throughout the world, companies have to adapt as soon as possible to new techniques, new competitors and erratic financial flows, which usually act to the detriment of employment. This is what generally happens in large concerns, where work is reorganised to reach productivity objectives, or highly capital-intensive production systems are introduced to meet the quality standards required by world markets.

78.   The rapid rise in productivity, especially in industry, has led some observers to maintain that the jobs coefficient has been decreasing permanently of late. ILO

---

[59]   PROKOPENKO, Joseph, *La gestión de la productividad,* Manual Práctico, Ginebra,OIT, 1989, pág. 3-4.
[60]   Idem, pág. 264.

researchers do not bear out this hypothesis, mainly because the number of jobs has increased very swiftly in other sectors, especially in services. However, there has been a growing polarisation of labour markets, as nowadays higher qualifications are demanded. At the same time, the need to abate costs has brought about a proliferation of low remunerated, badly protected and frequently transient work posts. As a result of all this, the de-structuring of the economy has gone hand in hand with the growth of technically very complex production systems.

79.　In many countries, structural readjustment and new competitive advantages seem to lead to a constant restructuring of large enterprises, which may cause a reduction of their payroll. Such payroll contractions have been affecting millions of workers. Many current studies show that the way in which this is done often cuts back the companies' operations and achievements, and brings about new cuts in personnel which, in the opinion of many high executives, undermine the confidence of the companies' workers and diminish productivity.

80.　In most economies, the greatest number of jobs is concentrated in the services sector. This has become more marked in the last few decades, both in the United States, Latin America and the Caribbean. On the other hand, it has been proved that the average output per employee is higher in industry than in services, and also grows more quickly. The slow growth of output per worker in the services sector means a lessening of the average productivity of the economy and of the intersectoral productivity gaps. The latter might imply an increase of wage differentials, affecting income distribution among the employed population.

81.　In such contexts, social policies are liable to become a productive factor by contributing to boost productivity and improving the social situation. It is for that reason that the ILO is systematising data to show that the quality of employment can be profitable by itself as a result of progress in productivity. In this manner a more solid, scientific base will be developed to settle conflicts or apparent mutual concessions between the "quantity" and the "quality" of work posts. At the same time, the notion is being advanced that there are two critical factors in the simultaneous search for decent work and the improvement of productivity: first, investing in theoretical and practical knowledge and, second, jobs without hazards, by means of safety and health at work.

82.　Governments can also generate employment by expanding social services. Investing in sectors such as health, education, nutrition and technical and vocational training, they create social employment. More immediately, they are creating work posts for the teaching and health personnel of the countries. But there are also the long-term results: a healthier, better educated and well-qualified population is the most reliable tool to raise productivity and improve living standards.

83.   When the time comes to formulate policies, some considerations are in order. Work productivity in Latin America and the Caribbean is low by international standards, and shows significant and growing divergences among sectors in the various countries. At international level, available studies show that the average productivity in the Region is about a third of that in the U.S. For instance, making a motor car in Brazil and Mexico takes 40 and 48 hours' work, whereas a similar unit is turned out with 25 hours in the U.S. and 17 hours in Japan. Internally, the sector of micro-enterprises concentrates 25% of the non-agricultural employment of the Region, and has a productivity per worker that is barely over 15% of that of the modern sector of the economy. Consequently, it is not only necessary to increase overall productivity but also to reduce differentials among the different sectors.

84.   Small firms and enterprises are playing an increasingly important role in production systems, as part of chains of suppliers, local networks of producers or low-productivity solutions for those who do not have access to jobs in the informal sector. Although large communities greatly contribute to create employment, it is really small enterprises that generate the majority of work posts. They may be just one person working by himself/herself in the informal sector, or complex production units with dozens of wage earners. Many of these work posts provide a stable income and work environment, but there are also many unsatisfactory work posts, with low productivity, dangerous or lacking the most elementary social protection.

Vocational training and competitiveness strategies

85.   With increasing frequency, vocational training is mentioned as an essential component of strategies to improve competitiveness. In a literal sense, the term competitiveness refers to the capacity of an enterprise, sector or country to compete in an economic framework. Although that meaning has always been accepted, it is of particular importance in these times of economic globalisation, when trade opening processes make the strengths and weaknesses of economic players even more evident.

86.   In any case, there are different notions as to which strategies are the most adequate, and above all, what combination of measures can be most effective. On the one hand, there are examples of strategies based fundamentally on macro-economic measures that tend to abate production costs, such as decisions regarding exchange rate policies, tax exemptions or reduction of labour costs (wages, lay-offs, etc.). On the other hand, (and not necessarily in contradiction with other measures), efforts are made pointing to a broader horizon, to what has been called "systemic competitiveness".

87.   One of the main differences between these two approaches lies in the time scope of their policies. The first approach is usually adopted in order to get more or less immediate results, in adverse circumstances. The typical and most usual example is to resort to a devaluation of the national currency in order to inject dynamics into the export sector, either unilaterally or in response to similar measures by other States. Such decisions have an almost immediate effect, for which reason they are the most frequent strategy to increase competitiveness.

88.   The systemic competitiveness version is aimed instead at long-term results. It does not depend on a limited and relatively straightforward series of measures, but on a wide variety of policies that will jointly result in a more competitive overall situation for the economy. Policies for investing in public and private infrastructures, technological innovation and development, integration of sectors and productive chains, investing in the development of human capital (education and training) are some of the typical instruments proposed by this approach.

89.   It is precisely in this second approach that vocational training has a more clear-cut and central role. On the basis that investing to upgrade people's qualifications is of itself an action that favours competitiveness, it in turn reinforces other lines of complementary policy. Although vocational training is a useful option in any context, its beneficial contributions to society and the economy are most evident in long-term strategic approaches.

90.   It is also evident that insofar as vocational training may take a prominent position in long-term strategies, it has to face the challenge of rethinking itself and in its relation with other fields of activity in strategic terms. In that respect, two generalised over-simplifications are on their way out in the Region.

91.   The first of them is the concept that vocational training was a limited period in people's existence, that usually preceded their active life. Although this issue is analysed in greater detail in the following section, we may point out here that at present, and in line what is happening in other parts of the world, in Latin America and the Caribbean vocational training is seen as more of a permanent process, necessary all along people's life, and not just a preparatory stage for filling in a specific work post.

92.   Secondly, the idea of vocational training as a specialised and in a way self-sufficient field of activity, is also losing ground to the concept that it is an inter-disciplinary and inter-institutional jurisdiction and must, as such, be viewed in the framework of integral strategies that attend to the economy, productive sectors and chains, enterprises and the community at large.

49

93.   Consequently, vocational training is aiming at two kinds of integration: in a vertical (or diachronic) sense, insofar as it tries to provide answers not just for specific situations, but to the transformation thereof (lifelong training); and in a transversal (or synchronous) sense, where it looks for co-ordination with other fields of social and economic policy, with other institutional spheres and disciplines.

94.   Those are, in sum, the two fundamental dimensions of a process of transformation of vocational training, that is shifting it towards the bounds of a strategic and functional horizon, in search of -among other things- systemic competitiveness.

Quality management in vocational training

95.   Concerns about quality are as old in the production of goods and services as in training activities. Ensuring the quality of training has been an age-old consideration of Latin American and Caribbean vocational training institutions. At present, the role of quality has evolved in the same way as the role and expectations of the institutions themselves.

96.   In a decent work approach, people are not trained to pass an exam, but for their whole work in life. The quality of the training lies in recognising participants for the personal individuals they are. Hence that stress is laid on incorporating abilities for communication, participation, teamwork, negotiation and the exchange of ideas, all of which are associated with a wide range of labour and social participation possibilities

97.   Rather than just ensuring the achievement of certain academic goals -usually scored by theoretical/practical assessments- the concept of quality in training has been built around the effectiveness it may have to instil into participants serviceable abilities for their labour ad social life. The **UNESCO "Delors Report"** (1996) spelled out the four main pillars, or tasks, of learning: learning to learn; learning to do, learning to live with others, and learning to be. Quality thus becomes a complex, diverse and holistic concept that that cannot be gauged by traditional evaluation tests.

98.   The ever greater number and diversity of actors on the supply side of training, the new forms of financing and the necessary relevance demanded of training programmes are, among others, some of the factors that have sparked off processes of modernisation and transformation in training bodies. Such procedures have nowadays high priority on their agendas.

99. On the other hand, training users want to know about the best offers, those that guarantee the greatest efficiency. Both employers and workers are on the lookout for signs of efficiency. Providers of funds are also interested in the best possible use of the resources they have invested. Institutions with a quality management constitute a social guarantee to the efficiency of public expenditure in training. The same reasoning applies to funds from the private sector: they should be handed to bodies capable of accounting for relevant, efficient and effective training processes. Vocational training institutions are therefore interested in improving the efficiency and relevance of their activities, which has been recently reflected in their adoption of management mechanisms to ensure quality.

100. Some institutions take part in national evaluation and quality control mechanisms in their centres and other operating units, and participate in surveys implemented in their countries. Such is the case of the **Instituto Nacional de Aprendizaje, INA** (National Training Institute) which recently was awarded top marks in an evaluation procedure conducted by the **Sistema Nacional de Evaluación, SINE** (National Evaluation System) among 29 public institutions in **Costa Rica.**

101. Others adopt mechanisms, define indicators or devise systems for grading results that may ensure the quality of their response. Such is the case of the evaluation system utilised by **SENAI** of Brazil, that grants Gold, Silver and Bronze awards to its Model Centres of Vocational Education and National Technology Centres. Along similar lines, and within a modernisation process, the **INTECAP** of Guatemala has adopted the 5 "S" system to promote a quality culture.

102. There are also institutes that take part in national quality drives and work in association with national standardisation and accreditation bodies. This joint work is evidenced by the accreditation of those institutes' Technological Centres to offer metrology or testing services for compliance with quality standards by a number of products in national and international markets. Such is the case of the **SENAI National Technology Centres (Brazil)** and of the **SENA Technological Development Centres (Colombia).** Along similar lines are training and enterprise counselling activities for the implementation of quality systems, an increasingly frequent service supplied by training institutions, as happens in the **Service Centres for Small and Medium Enterprises** of the **SENATI (Peru),** that stress quality enhancement.

103. At the same time, training institutions have looked for an external quality stamp and have resorted to quality certification, that is usually audited and verified by an external organisation under the ISO-9000 family of standards.

104. New experiences of certified quality management in vocational training are to be found from Central America to the Southern Cone. The following are some examples:

51

• The **Servicio Nacional de Aprendizaje Industrial, SENAI** (National Training Institute) of **Brazil** accounts for one of the first experiences in the Region, that started in the **State of Santa Catarina** with the application of the 5 "S" programme and subsequent ISO-9000 certification in 1997 by the German firm TUV RHEINLAND. The SENAI regional departments of Paraná, Espíritu Santo and Pernambuco have also ISO 9000 certifications. The Service's National Direction at Brasilia has recently adopted a quality guarantee system with the following coverage: Planning, Development and Co-ordination of Strategic Projects and Operational Improvement Projects.

• SENAI also has an internal system for quality acknowledgement of its Training Centres that, through an evaluation process grants them the title of "**Model Centres of Vocational Education**" or "**National Technology Centres**". The system is based on the criteria of the National Quality Programme, that includes: Process Management, Persons' Management, Leadership, Strategic Management, Focusing on clients and markets, Information Results and Management. It has three successive levels of compliance, in ascending order: Bronze, Silver and Gold.

• In **Peru**, the **Servicio Nacional de Adiestramiento Técnico Industrial, SENATI** (Industrial and Technical Training Service) was awarded the ISO 9001 quality certification. After a widespread national effort, this institution obtained that certification for the following Vocational Training Programmes: Dual Apprenticeship, Qualification of Workers in Service, Industrial Technicians, Industrial Managers, Industrial Masters, Engineering Technician, Ongoing Training, Multimedia Training, Information Science and Labour Grants. In practically all SENATI zone centres, Technical Fabrication Services, Non-destructive Testing and Counselling for Small and Medium Enterprises have also been certified.

• After adopting a number of measures for institutional modernisation -which among other things opened up the Institute for accreditation by other public and private training bodies, the INA of **Costa Rica** started a quality management process, and in January 1999 obtained the certification of its Accreditation Unit by **INTECO** and the **Spanish Standardisation and Certification Association (AENOR)** according to ISO 9002 Standard.

• The **Consejo de Normalización y Certificación de Competencia Laboral, CONOCER** (Labour Competencies Standardisation and Certification Council), of **Mexico,** was awarded an ISO quality certification standard in February 2000, for the adoption of efficient systems to ensure the quality of its processes in the design, development production and distribution of its products, and in ancillary services.

• The **SENCE** of **Chile** was the first public service in that country to obtain a quality certification of the ISO 9000 family. In January of this year it was awarded a certificate accrediting that "the process of Constitution of Technical Training Institutes in the Metropolitan Region "complies with the requirements of ISO 9002 quality standards".

• In line with its modernisation programme, the Instituto Técnico de Capacitación y Productividad, **INTECAP (Technical Institute for Training and Productivity)** of **Guatemala** has taken a number of measures to develop a "culture of overall quality" in the Institute. They include a clear definition of the institution's vision and mission, and adoption of the programme known as 5 "S", a management philosophy that lies at the base of overall quality.

Training along life

105. Nowadays, the educational nature of vocational training is emphasised in accepting that it comes together with other teaching modes and branches to meet the challenge of fulfilling people's need for a lifelong education.

106. The barriers between manual and non-manual tasks and between thought and action have been modified. What gives persons a general knowledge that they can transfer to work is a balanced combination of fundamental know-how, technical skills and social aptitudes. Consequently, it is possible to start contributing to the mastery of the basic codes of modernity from elementary school on, and it is essential to turn the teaching-learning process into a continuum.

107. This continuum in turn gives rise to another one between formal education, vocational and technical training, and informal learning, making up a vertical axis around which a person's whole life revolves. Additionally, there is a horizontal axis wherein all living spaces become educational environments.

108. The lifelong education approach rests upon the following: firstly on the need to keep up competitiveness in a world of constantly changing products and technologies; secondly, on the rapid obsolescence of knowledge and the demystification of professions (entailing the loss of power and prestige of diplomas and the revaluation of real competencies), and thirdly, on the need to struggle against unemployment, as a way of reducing the exclusion or marginalisation that stem from social stratification and/or segregation for reasons of age, culture, region, ethics or gender, that characterise vulnerable populations.

109. It is therefore a priority to give people the means to manage their own labour and occupational development, find their first job, look for a new one, start up a business, retrain through courses, and instruct themselves permanently, whether employed or unemployed, at home or in their place of work. This changeover in training, that is both conceptual and practical, implies a number of consequences that have to be underlined:

• In the first place, as opposed to what happened a few decades ago, when the trend was towards specialisation, now it seems increasingly necessary for persons to master a number of basic and general skills, enabling them both to perform in less controlled work environments with unforeseen situations that must be solved as they go along, and to "surf" in a difficult and competitive labour market. Specific training, which is still required, is obtained on the job, and sometimes enterprises prefer to take charge of it. Training bodies, and many training programmes, are gradually getting nearer to general or regular education, regarding both contents and institutions. As regular education is also undergoing a reform process, it benefits from this rapprochement, insofar as vocational training furnishes it with experience in relating to the productive sector. In other words, this is a profitable synergy for both traditions and institutions.

• Secondly, the responsibility for training is now beginning to be shared, and necessarily provides an opportunity for agreement and co-operation. If people are no longer learning exclusively in educational centres, but also at home and at work, the responsibility for training is shared by training bodies, employers, governments and the individuals themselves (and the organisations that represent them). Tripartite management is revitalised, and the emergence of new forms of training management is favoured. These new approaches do not adhere to singe models: for instance, they may be social or political accords allowing for the development of dual (alternating) training models, or training / production centres managed jointly with entrepreneurial chambers or trade unions. There are foundations run by trade unions and financed by employers, as well as national training systems managed on a tripartite basis. But whatever shape they may adopt, the general trend is towards alliances to take advantage of the resources provided by the various actors, to use them more efficiently in the service of the ongoing and overall training of citizens.

• Thirdly, the very nature of lifelong training dictates that in order to exist, it requires a very flexile and dynamic offer. As a result of the gradual blurring of borderlines between productive branches in regard of basic skills, there are infinite possibilities in the paths followed by individuals to get the same type of job. The different training demands of those persons can hardly be standardised. The best option is to offer them a sort of "help yourself" menu, where each one can pick to meet their training needs in different circumstances and deadlines, with varying degrees of depth and different contents. On the other hand, training demands have also expanded and diversified under the influence of aspects such as: the greater relative weight of the knowledge factor in production; the entry of large contingents into active life (specially in the less industrialised countries); the shrinking of public employment; the number of displaced workers from companies that are being revamped or have disappeared; or the emergence of new forms of employment and self-employment. Looking after all the employed or unemployed active population of the modern sector and of the other more backward sectors, whether formal or informal, young or adult, is not a task that can be tackled efficiently by a single agent, even with large financial resources (which is not a frequent situation).

Here again, there is nothing for it but to co-ordinate efforts through the concerted action of different actors who, with their own resources, may help to build up a sufficiently broad, flexible and diverse training system to deal with an increasingly heterogeneous demand for lifelong training.

110. In **Argentina,** a reform of technical education started in 1996 that has resulted in the implementation of "**Trayectos Técnicos Profesionales**", **TTP** ("Technical Occupational Itineraries"), optional training offers for all students or graduates of the so-called "polymodal" education. The purpose of TTPs is to train technicians in specific occupational areas requiring the mastery of competencies that can only be developed through long, systematic training processes. The very design of these Itineraries is an interesting and current example of the endeavours to bring different educational and training systems together:

• *Polymodal education,* because it is a combination of training alternatives covering wide areas of knowledge and social and productive activities (a total of five modalities) the choice of which enables students to consolidate fundamental skills on the basis of problems linked to their interests and motivations. TTPs offer the possibility of occupational induction in areas calling for specific technological and vocational competencies.

• *Vocational training,* because TTPs supplement a training offer that in Argentina appears aimed at the development of skills that are required for performing in certain jobs and/or constitute components of active employment policies intended to promote the access to labour of groups with specific needs.

• *Permanent and higher education and training,* since the objective of TTPs is to launch students on an occupational course, ensuring their access to a base of knowledge and abilities that may equip them to start off with a first job in a given area, and to continue learning throughout their active life. The idea is that the training imparted through TTPs should supplement other educational alternatives, in order to allow for subsequent stages of evolution, specificity, retraining and - possibly- changing over to another occupation.

111. In **Brazil,** the **Plano Nacional de Qualificação do Trabalhador, PLANFOR** (National Plan for Workers' Qualification) that is being implemented since 1995 by the former **Secretaría de Formación y Desarrollo Profesional, SEFOR**[61] (Secretariat for Training and Occupational Development) of the Ministry of Labour, has appeared as a proposal to inject new dynamics into the training programmes financed by the Fund for the Protection of Workers -FAT-. It also pursues the explicit objective of dealing with vocational training as a public policy, recognising and mobilising new training actors and building up a new institutionality for the country's occupational education.

[61] As from recent restructuring, this body was renamed Secretariat for Employment Public Policies (Portuguese acronym SPPE)

PLANFOR is structured along three main guidelines:

• Conceptual advancement. This implies the development and consolidation of a new methodological and operational approach to vocational education envisaging the following dimensions:

Focus on the demand of the labour market and the productive profile of the target population, oriented by the effective demand of the productive sector and gathering together the interests and needs of workers, employers, communities.
Rights of the productive citizen, considered on a permanent, continuous basis, complementary in nature (never a substitute) to elementary education (of first and second degree) that is a constitutional right of citizens.
Overall development of basic, specific and/or management abilities in workers, by means of courses, counselling, and other presential or distance activities.
Consideration of the social, economic and regional diversity of the economically active population (EAP), by promoting equal opportunities in training programmes and in access to the labour market.

• Institutional co-ordination. Implies singling out, co-ordinating and developing the main important actors in a public policy for work and income generation. Consolidation of a national vocational training network for the ongoing training of the EAP, on a participative and decentralised basis. The Vocational Education Network to be made up by the effective or potential offer of public or private entities of a national or international kind, governmental or non-governmental, including at least the following institutions: universities, federal, state and municipal technical schools, employers' foundations and organisations, the "S System" in particular, trade unions and workers' organisations; independent vocational schools, community societies and other lay or religious organisations.

• Support of civil society. Full scale promotion of workers' training activities, including not only training courses but also counselling, extension services, research and studies. Although such action is addressed to the EAP, it guarantees priority for vulnerable groups (insofar as FAT funds are concerned). Vulnerability is defined as a combination of factors such as poverty, low schooling, gender, race and colour, special needs and other conditions hampering access to, or permanence, in the labour market and other alternatives of occupational training.

112. The **Secretaría de Educación Media Técnica, SEMTEC** of the **Ministry of Education of Brazil** designed a proposal for a **System of Vocational Education Based on Competencies,** conceived as a social opportunity mechanism, promoting the process of evaluation and certification of occupational competencies with a view to concluding and finishing studies. The system recognises that persons acquire skills in different contexts, not just at school, and that such skills may

recognised and certified for occupational purposes, or to continue studies and obtain a diploma.

Objectives of the system are: evaluating and certifying competencies developed by individuals, regardless of the way in which they were acquired, for purposes of vocational education, with a view to continuing or finishing a technical course. Evaluating and certifying competencies required for jobs and occupations characteristic of the basic level of vocational education. Promoting educational development, the improvement of workers' levels of learning and occupational recognition.

Some of the fundamental principles of the system are: effective participation by employers and workers at all levels; permanent co-ordination between education and labour; flexibility: democratisation of access; inclusion of workers, and occupational recognition.

113. Also in **Brazil** there is another example of integration of the vocational training and higher education systems through the offer of tertiary level courses by SENAI. Some of them are higher courses on the following subjects: Environmental Technology, Graphic Technology, Mecatronics Technology, Clothing Technology, Industrial Automation Technology, and Textile Industrial Engineering.

114. In **Chile,** the **Programa de Educación y Capacitación Permanente** (Permanent Education and Training Programme) depends on the Ministry of Education and the Ministry of Labour and Social Security. It is intended to expand ongoing education and training opportunities in support of the country's economic and social transformation, to help achieve greater economic competitiveness and social equity (integration and promotion), and to meet the growing need of people to learn and get trained throughout life. All this to be done through offering new opportunities for ongoing education and training, improving technical education and facilitating access and re-entry into the labour market for young persons and adults, and creating instruments for a lifelong learning process.

115. The Programme seeks to benefit the poorer sectors of the active population, who are already employed or looking for a job, and wish to upgrade their occupational skills and their literacy and schooling levels through education and training. Regarding those excluded from the training system, the Programme will give special support to efforts for the incorporation and use of new information and communication technologies in small and micro enterprises.

Another line of action points to bolstering the development of technical training by promoting co-operation between secondary and higher education and training, the training of teachers and instructors, support of curricular changes in secondary-level technical vocational schools, and access of Programme graduates into the labour market.

The Programme likewise intends to develop mechanisms enabling persons to certify progress itineraries in their technical careers (regardless of where and how they have acquired their competencies); systems guaranteeing the quality of training offers; and a scheme of information and guidance on the labour market and training opportunities.

116. In **Mexico,** the **Consejo Nacional de Educación para la Vida y el Trabajo** (National Council of Education for Life and Work) was created in the year 2000 as part of the action suggested in the document **Basic Considerations for the 2001-2006 Sectoral Education Programme.** The long-term objective of this project is devising a new scheme for the educational attention of young people and adults. The fundamental purpose is that all Mexican men and women over the age of 15 may have -along their lives- the capacity and opportunity of embarking upon ascending spirals of learning, in order to acquire new knowledge, abilities, attitudes and values enabling them to face the decisions that affect the conditions of their daily life... This will also improve their labour performance and civic participation, and it will lead to a fuller existence.

The gist of the proposal is a new educational conception. The proposition is based, on the one hand, not only on the economic but also political, social and cultural challenges and requirements faced by mankind in general and Mexico in particular, as a result of the stunning changes in technology, information science and communication, and on the other hand on the evolution of thinking in that connection.

This conception implies retrieving and integrating multiple educational dimensions, some of them with a long history of systematic action and national scope, others offered in a scattered and incipient way (literacy campaigns, compulsory elementary education, occupational training). It also has explicit educational goals, such as the acquisition of basic learning skills, which include a new and much needed "technological and digital literacy"; ongoing occupational training along life, civic instruction, particularly regarding human rights and democratic procedures; education for improving daily life conditions in such important aspects as health and reproduction, the prevention of addictions, emotional relations within the family, self esteem and self knowledge, or more immediate topics like improvement of home economics, personal realisation and affluence.

As potential target group, the project has identified all the Mexican population over the age of 15. It acknowledges the fact that it is a heterogeneous group requiring focalised solutions incorporating knowledge into various daily procedures.

117. In **Honduras,** the **Programa de Educación para el Trabajo, POCET** (Programme of Education for Work) is a Central American example of this process of rapprochement between regular education systems (specially adults' education) and training, in a framework of lifelong learning. It is one of the first and most fruitful examples in the country of integration between traditions that historically had few common links, and lacked experience in the recent debates about the interconnections across the board and other paradigms, particularly education throughout life. Joint action has been taken by the **Honduran Secretariat for Public Education,** and the **Instituto Nacional de Formación Profesoinal, INFOP** (National Vocational Training Institute), with methodological approaches that are usually only possible for non-governmental organisations.

The POCET Programme constitutes the pivot of a whole tradition built around the principles of adults' education, with an emphasis on assistance and literacy. It led the way in bringing together the contributions made by all those involved in the people's education, with other streams -like vocational training- that had a long experience in the field of education for productive work, and were all very much concerned about the advent of new paradigms of production and labour and changes in the employment market, and the continued existence of groups and sectors afflicted by exclusion situations.

118. In the **Dominican Republic,** the **Instituto Nacional de Formación Técnico Profesional, INFOTEP** (National Institute for Technical-Vocational Training), in its recently adopted **strategic plan INFOTEP ACCIÓN 2005,** embarks upon the implementation of an innovative and flexible curricular system, that may be assimilated with other educational sub-systems, to meet the current needs of the labour market. An initial strategy in that respect, is to promote the creation of inter-institutional working committees, forums and discussion groups to make curricular standardisation viable, and favour the horizontal and vertical inter-connection among the various sub-systems and for skills' certification purposes. As a second strategy, INFOTEP intends to develop training methodologies on the basis of occupational competencies' standards and non-traditional systems, in order to respond in a more dynamic and flexible manner to the changes and demands of the national and international labour markets.

119. In **Uruguay,** an overall educational reform was started in 1995 whose main guidelines are the attainment of equity and the improvement of quality. In the technical-vocational field, the reform aims at a consistent technical and technological education. It should be well co-ordinated and of high quality, looking after its own specific objectives (i.e. providing an efficient and polyvalent training that may help in the transformation of productive structures and improve the living conditions of workers) and also complementing regular secondary schools, in order to offer people an integral intermediate education. For that purpose, the **Consejo de Educación**

Técnico Profesional, CETP-UTU (Technical-Vocational Education Council), has restructured and reformulated its educational offer. Main novelties are a Basic Technological Cycle and a Technology Bachelor. The first one resorts to various methods to make adolescents internalise a technological culture and develop the competencies that will serve them as a basis for subsequent broader and modern vocational options. The Technological Bachelors' courses, of three years' duration, have a twofold goal. They can be a terminal stage in secondary studies, leading to the certificate of Technical Assistant, but they are also supposed to equip students with a repertory of intellectual, technical and manual abilities. Their contents are interdisciplinary, organised round a central core, covering the main areas of development of the national economy and built upon job clusters. Graduates can go into the University or continue further specialised studies in the CETP itself, an organisation that trains middle and high technicians to meet the demands of the productive sectors.

The objectives of this reform have been very explicit. It is intended to provide young people with a sound general education, a good scientific and technological grounding, and the knowledge, abilities and skills needed for flexibility, swift adaptation to change and continuous learning. Uruguay is a small developing country in a world of constant economic, scientific and technological change. Its educational challenge is to prepare its human resources and its economy to live in a state of uncertainty. Consequently, the symbolic languages its people need to master go beyond a capacity for oral and written communication: they include computerisation, telecommunications, foreign languages and the critical interpretation of audio-visual messages. Also essential is the mastery of scientific methods and knowledge in order to comprehend, interpret and manage natural and social phenomena; of mathematical skills, to acquire methodologies for identifying problems and solving them. Social and historical notions have to be modified, as cultural borders and global geography become imprecise, and satellite communications radically alter the management of information. Last but not least, the young must acquire a technological culture that may facilitate their integration into the world of production and labour and to understand its technical and social dimensions.

The occupational competencies' approach

120. A lifelong education requires mechanisms that make it possible to establish a learning continuum. Of recent importance among them is the "occupational competencies' movement", that is completely transforming the way of conceiving education. By competency we understand a person's real capacity to achieve an expected objective in a given labour situation. The idea of competency is closely associated with innovation in soft technologies, and with new skills profiles.

121. At present we think that persons are competent when they have a repertory of abilities, knowledge and skills, and the capacity to use them adaptively in a variety of labour contexts and organisations. Reasoned knowledge is assumed, as there is no true competency unless theoretical knowledge is accompanied by the qualities and capacity enabling persons to carry out the decisions dictated by that competency itself. Personal attitudes are also involved, and the affective side of individuals.

122. The taylorist/fordist model was clearly prescriptive: workers were considered to be qualified insofar as they proved their capacity to comply with a previously established outside standard of behaviour. Nowadays, workers have the dilemma of managing a situation, making complex decision at the very moment of action, assuming personal responsibility before unforeseen situations. All this implies a social involvement that strongly mobilises their intelligence and subjectivity.

123. Present conditions call for the notion of competency, which is inseparable from action and tested by problem solving. Competency appears as a valuable tool for training people because:

• it vindicates the conjunction of knowledge, understanding and abilities mea-sured in terms of performance, or capacity to ensure the necessary co-ordination and complementation between basic education and the various forms of occupa-tional training (offered by specific institutions, organised and systematic training by employers, on-the-job training, community action, etc.);
• it allows for the recognition and certification of learning regardless of how and when it was acquired, and supports the relevance, quality and upgrading of curricular contents and teachers' training.

124. In a world where knowledge is valued as the main source of competitiveness, a good training system is required, generating knowledge of immediate application in people's employment and life. Any training oriented towards the generation of competencies for employability has to find new ways of identifying current occupa-tional profiles.

125. Performance based on competencies is not just a description of the tasks and operations carried out by workers. It has to include the contribution it makes to the achievement of entrepreneurial objectives and, in consequence, the training needs that the training system has to fulfil. Identification of the new competencies required for access to work makes the training subsequently imparted highly ef-fective.

126. Procedures of dialogue and collective elaboration by workers and employers have proved to be effective for the identification of new competencies. It is no

longer necessary to demonstrate that it is the workers who can best explain and understand the everyday problems of their trade. In view of this reality, a decent job is also that allowing for the collective identification, creation and improvement of the processes and results obtained. Decent work necessitates organisations integrating workers in the definition of training needs. Training and dialogue, training and negotiation: in that manner the link is forged between training and decent work.

127. Over and above identifying the competencies required by the new corporate structures, training programmes must assume new characteristics in accordance with current challenges. Training has to become more flexible, recognise the different places where people learn, and know how much time persons have for learning.

128. The gradual blurring of labour practices that grew mainly during the so-called "industrialised economy" is giving rise to new scenarios in training demand. Workers need to have time-flexible training offers to fit in with their schedules. Their available time for study is no longer compatible with the fixed timetables of traditional training programmes. Decent work requires flexible programmes regarding time and location.

129. To a large extent, competencies are developed at work. Consequently, a decent job is increasingly becoming a place for learning. Training has to take into account labour contexts as generators of competencies, so that through dignified work, people may have access to open certification mechanisms for the competencies acquired by education or from experience, or a mixture of both.

130. We first talked of contextual flexibility. Training has to be delivered in a number of non-schoolroom contexts. The work place and the home are nowadays learning environments. The traditional classroom and teaching workshop are no longer the only places where competencies can be developed. Individual learn from experience, they learn at home, and training must recognise that fact and take advantage of it. Training and decent work imply a flexible, non-school kind of training.

131. The new characteristics of employment are also conferring a new meaning upon the use of time for training. People get trained and develop competencies in different places, and therefore, at different moments. Traditionally set school hours have been disrupted by the varying time availability of modern workers. Access to training should not depend on the predetermined capability of training institutions, but on the needs of those who have to develop their competencies.

132. Training providers are starting to make their programmes more flexible in terms of contexts and times. The new training offer must break away from the

traditional paradigm of learning in the schoolroom at fixed times, and acknowledge the various sources of learning tapped by persons who have to reconcile their social and personal existence with their work.

133. It is also necessary to assess knowledge according to the level of competencies that persons have accumulated. If they learn in different contexts and at different times, mechanisms for evaluation and accreditation must be readily available to them, and not confined to the "formal" moments of the training process. In consequence, mechanisms are required to evaluate and certify persons' competencies in a transparent and objective manner. The degree of complexity of training is no longer judged by its duration, but by the occupational skills and abilities it may impart to candidates.

134. In summary, training in an environment that may favour decent work should endeavour clearly to dispense the competencies required for successful performance. It should develop programmes aiming at such competencies, and promote the creation of transparent and comprehensive certification systems. It should also be as open as possible to access (flexibility of contexts and time), so as to further disseminate the concept of decent work. The idea is to build up training systems facilitating people's entry and re-entry into the labour market along life.

135. As proclaimed by the recent Report of the ILO Director General, it is necessary to formulate training policies including measures that may enhance the capability of workers to perform in the changing conditions of current reality. The concept of training has been radically altered, particularly with regard to contents, which will now be more worker-friendly insofar as they will be recognised by more than one enterprise. The increased value of "portable" competencies will enhance workers' employment possibilities.

136. The training offer is no longer identified with a single leading institution or agency. Quite the contrary: it is now associated with an array of co-ordinated services supplied by the State, Ministries of Education and Labour, Employers' Organisations and Trade Unions, among others.

137. However, this greater abundance of training agents, and the efforts that are generally being made for the sake of change and modernisation, affect the very concept and effectiveness of training. The participating actors require support, as do those in charge of formulating policies in the area of development and training of human resources, so that they may better equipped to generate training programmes, get acquainted with the best practices and learn about current experiences.

138. Along those lines, the occupational competencies' approach has been prominent in most of the training activities implemented by vocational institutions, minis-

tries of labour, ministries of education, employers and trade unions throughout the Region.

139. Vocational Training Institutions in the Region have been trying out their hand at evolving occupational profiles based on competencies. They have also been updating their training curricula and refining their evaluation instruments. For that purpose, social dialogue has been promoted and links have been established between employers and workers, with a view to devising more relevant and accessible training programmes. The following institutions may be enumerated in this connection: in Central America **INSAFORP** of **El Salvador, INTECAP** of **Guatemala, INA** of **Costa Rica.** In the Caribbean, **INFOTEP** of the **Dominican Republic** and the **National Training Agencies (NTAs)** of **Barbados, Jamaica** and **Trinidad & Tobago.** In South America, the competencies' approach is already being utilised by the **SENA** of **Colombia, INCE** of **Venezuela, SENATI** of **Peru, SENAI** of **Brazil, INFOCAL** of **Bolivia,** and others.

140. In **Brazil,** opening up to the international market has increased the demand for high-quality products, and consequently for highly qualified workers. The **SEFOR** of the **Ministry of Labour** and the ILO, are jointly implementing a project for the design of a certification system. The diversity of the training offer in the country, and the interaction of many actors in a scenario where training is being dispensed not only in the institutional environment of the "S system" (SENAI, SENAC, SENAR, SENAT) but also by a large number of other private institutes connected with communities or sectors, has created a situation in which occupational certification can make things transparent, facilitate workers' mobility and improve the quality of training.

The project is taking into account the whole range of vocational training experiences in Brazil, from those run by NGOs and trade unions, to the ones of the "S system". Introduction of the competencies' approach is a critical aspect of the proposal the scheme may submit. Several international models have been analysed in that connection; the experiences of Brazilian enterprises have also been identified and disseminated.

The project developed several products, like a survey of the most important experiences in occupational certification in Brazil and the preparation of two technical manuals on the qualitative analysis of work, and evaluation of competencies. A technical group was also formed that has been carrying out certification activities in the framework of **INMETRO,** the **Brazilian Metrology and Standardisation Institute.**

In fact, the project has triggered a strong flow of social dialogue, with the participation of several trade union associations, representatives of training bodies, SEMTEC, and private companies interested in improving certification systems.

141. A special feature of this undertaking is the participation of SEMTEC, which implies a coming together of formal secondary education and vocational training. The framework provided by the new Brazilian Law of Basic Education Directives made it possible for SEMTEC to start work on certification and adoption of the competencies' approach. The objectives of education and labour have many things in common, and joint action is facilitating harmonisation.

142. In **Mexico,** the experience of the CONOCER started in 1995, and is the most extensive initiative in the Region in the field of certification of labour competencies. It responds to the Mexican Government's interest in getting the different actors to take part in the development of training based on competency standards, and the certification thereof.

The main components of the occupational competencies' system are the following:

• Defining technical standards of occupational competency by branch of activity or occupational group, by the social actors with government support.
• Establishing mechanisms for the evaluation, verification and certification of the knowledge, abilities and skills of individuals, regardless of the way in which they have been acquired, provided that they comply with the technical standards of competency.
• Turning the training offer into a flexible modular system based on competency standards, to enable individuals to move from one module to another, according to their needs.
• Creating demand incentives to promote the new system among the population and enterprises, endeavouring for equity in the handing out of training and certification opportunities, without overlooking the needs of marginalised groups.

In the establishment of a nation-wide system, more emphasis is to be laid on defining standards for the more general functions in the different economic branches, technological languages and occupational areas.

This initiative is ultimately intended to find a valid alternative for linking together the different modalities of education and training and the employment demand of the country. The challenge is to face the modernisation of the educational and occupational training systems, not only to adapt them to the new economic and technological conditions, but above all to make them accessible for all sectors of the population, and endow them with adequate and relevant contents, and the level of quality that the labour market requires. 45 Committees for the Standardisation of Occupational Competencies are at present in operation in Mexico, 57 pilot experiments are being run in different sectors of economic activity to promote certification, and 7 Certifying and 9 Evaluation Centres have been accredited. The first 120 Certificates of Occupational Competency were awarded on 13 December of last year.

143. The concern for employability and proper use of human talents has gradually brought about greater participation by Ministries of Labour in the implementation of training models that may fulfil needs, in the framework of active employment policies. From an initially quantitative intent, that focused on the need to remedy the situation of groups that were vulnerable to unemployment, another policy has been adopted. It does not leave aside the first approach, but it incorporates a qualitative ingredient aimed at delivering qualifications that may be of use all along a person's active life, rather than brief fragmentary courses of short duration and difficult follow-up.

144. The Ministries of Labour of Argentina, Chile, El Salvador and Uruguay are beginning to implement training and certification models. **Argentina** counts on proposals created from Instituto Nacional de Educación Tecnológica, INET (National Institute of Technological Education) and another one has been elaborated within the ILO destinated to the Ministry of Labour, Employment and Training of Human Resources. **Uruguay,** and **Chile** more recently, are formulating projects for the creation of systems for training and certification of competencies. The Ministry of Labour of **El Salvador** is closely involved in the development of a system of this kind by the Salvadoran training institute.

145. There are also instances of private companies that have incorporated the competency model for the management of their human resources. Cases of this kind are to be found in the automotive sector, the graphic industry, food processing and the pharmaceutical area, to name but a few.

146. In several countries, trade unions have been concerned to include in collective bargaining new aspects of labour relations, such as access to a relevant and ongoing training. Applications of the competencies' approach are now appearing, with the participation of workers and management representatives in the design and analysis of job profiles. All this in a joint effort, in one hand, to raise productivity and competitiveness, and on the other hand, the development of new ways or schemes of negotiation and dialogue between the union and the enterprise.

147. These efforts are leading to the development of a common language wherein the contribution of workers is valued by its results, and more transparent methods are used for recognising it, like the certification of competencies, whichever way they have been acquired. Thus, the road to decent work is built upon a relevant, flexible and adequate kind of training.

IV
VOCATIONAL TRAINING AS AN INSTRUMENT FOR SOCIAL PROTECTION

148. Enhancing the scope and efficiency of social protection for all is the third strategic objective of the ILO for the 2001-2002 biennium. Decent work, social security and working conditions are the main dimensions of this objective. From the point of view of vocational training and its potential contribution to this objective, consideration of certain social groups is of great importance, as their very social situation justifies prioritising action to increase and improve their levels of social protection. The present Chapter broaches on the one hand, the current situation of unemployed workers, of active workers who face processes of change and technological and productive recycling, of young persons and of women. On the other hand, it tries to summarise experiences under way in the Region regarding policies addressing such groups.

Vocational training for unemployed workers

149. Among the broad and heterogeneous clientele of vocational training, unemployed workers are probably one of the categories that call for greater efforts in terms of formulating policies and strategies, in the Region and in the world. They constitute a critical challenge, not only because of the quantitative significance of the problem, but also because the unemployed are a group of great internal diversity.

150. In the first place, unemployment has different characteristics according to people's stage of life. The requirements of young persons looking for their first job in the labour market, differ from those of an adult worker that has been laid off, an even more so from those of an unemployed worker of a certain age.

151. People's qualification levels are also a factor for differentiation, and although there is a positive correlation between skills level and access to work, very often and specially among the young, unemployment rates are significantly higher than those of the rest of the active population, despite the better schooling of the former.

152. Finally, men and women are affected differently by this problem, not only regarding their respective rates, but mainly because of the resulting situations in either case.

153. The already mentioned association between higher levels of qualification and possibilities of access to a job, and the wages earned, are of themselves convincing arguments to promote investments in general education, and vocational training in particular.

154. We must, however, point out once more that education and vocational training alone cannot solve the whole problem, nor deal with its many aspects. The regional experience shows, precisely, the need not just to increase and improve training action, but to try and co-ordinate it with complementary activities in an overall, systemic prospect.

155. For example, efforts to facilitate people's access into the labour market for the first time, should take into account not only the technical requirements of the market, but also the previous skills levels of the candidates, which in this case are mainly young persons and women. This leads to the consideration of whether training action by itself addresses the core of the problem, or it should be supplemented by some remedial or basic education measures. Another aspect that programmes for this kind of population usually take into account is, that one of the distinctive charcteristics of the first time labour searches is precisely the fact that it lacks prior labour experience. For that reason, training is frequently complemented with mechanisms to facilitate access to work, such as internships or grants.

156. Regarding workers that have been laid off, the most innovative experiences tend to incorporate social security mechanisms like unemployment insurance and retraining courses, but also develop comprehensive strategies that look after the whole situation that affects these people. As indicated earlier, unemployment brings along a number of consequences that go beyond the loss of regular earnings. When workers are cut off from their job, they also lose many of their forms of socialising. They feel their identity is blurred and their self-esteem undermined. These combined factors reinforce their feeling of being excluded, and if the situation persists, their possibilities of re-entering the labour market diminish.

157. Unemployment insurance and training opportunities are then supplemented by labour guidance and placement services, and by elementary education components whenever necessary. At the same time, to make up for the absence of socialising opportunities, the loss of identity and a sense of belonging, these experiences endeavour to provide individuals with collective spaces to search for solutions, and regain confidence in their own resources.

158. On the other hand, the new training strategies aimed at different kinds of unemployed persons, lay increasing stress no longer on strictly technical skills to perform as wage earners, but on the development of abilities of initiative and management, taking into account the alternatives of self-employment and micro-enterprises.

159. This is supported by reliable data that show the sustained decline of the classical forms of labour relations, and the finding that the only significant source of new employment are these modalities, where initiative and management are fundamental. Although very often micro-enterprises, as well as a many instances of self-employment, suffer from serious problems regarding productivity, social protection and remuneration, it is undeniable that they constitute one of the few economic areas where it is still possible to generate employment.

160. An important challenge stems from this, namely the design of strategies to strengthen micro-enterprises and self-employment, so that the job opportunities and source of income they represent may be economically more viable, with higher levels of productivity, social protection and higher earnings for the workers involved, They can thus become a key element in employment generation policies.

161. On the other hand, the new competencies required by the labour market tend towards a greater autonomy for workers -regardless of their contractual tie with employers- as they now have to manage their own occupational career. These new competencies are essential to deal successfully with the options of self-employment and productive undertakings, but they are also fundamental for any worker in the current labour market situation. Consequently, strategies aimed at developing a wide range of competencies exceeding the exclusively technical aspects of a job, and promoting the capacity to analyse, interpret, communicate, innovate and co-operate (among other things) are indispensable for all workers.

162. Finally, the problem of unemployment has some implications that we have not considered here yet. In the first place, unemployment has serious economic consequences for society in at least two ways: one, because unemployment insurance coverage and other protection mechanisms mean important costs (in proportion to the scope of unemployment); and two, because society is deprived of the contribution of the capacities of unemployed persons. In the second place, in he culture of our countries labour (and for decades in its most typical form, salaried employment), is the most direct way of having access to the full exercise of citizenship. It is therefore no exaggeration to say that, besides an economic problem of the first order, unemployment is also a political issue (and a challenge).

The training of active workers

163. Together with the attention paid to training strategies for the benefit of unemployed workers, the need is also stressed for action not just upon this ultimate manifestation of the problems afflicting economies and labour markets, but on the very causes thereof. In other words, unemployment itself is not the problem but its crudest expression or consequence. The chief problem is the incapacity of the economy to keep up or expand employment.

164. The practical result of the above is that, apart from offering training and other services to already idle workers, it is also necessary to act upon those who are still employed. This has, at least, a twofold effect:

• From the point of view of employers, as the capacities of active workers improve so does the contribution they can make to the productive and services organisations to which they belong, to boost both their productivity and competitiveness. This should help enterprises to improve their internal and market performance and consequently to maintain -and eventually raise- their level of employment.

• From the point of view of workers, they will benefit regarding their employability. They will be in a better position to deal with technological change, adapt to another work post in the same company, move about efficiently in the labour market to get other jobs, and in the last resort, face unemployment in better conditions.

165. In the longer view, the training of active workers is an essential component of lifelong education strategies. It is evident that training does not consist only of making people ready for active life, or retraining unemployed workers. Whether in historical retrospect or in a present-day view, it constitutes a continuum. Historically, persons do not only go through different stages with varying needs, but also find themselves in divergent labour relationships. Training should be capable to provide flexible answers to these different situations, through a multiplicity of resources and means. In a present-day context, society has different sectors and groups calling for diversified assistance services.

166. Furthermore, vocational training for active workers goes beyond their individual needs and those of enterprises. The concept of "organisational learning" that emerged in the late 1970's is now becoming widespread. It postulates basically that the enterprise of the future will no longer be able to confine itself to training persons for a job; it will have to organise work sequences in such a way that the whole organisation may learn.

167. The concept of organisational learning bolsters and complements the development of occupational competencies and the process of learning outside the

70

specific trade. It does not substitute organisational for individual learning, but rather harmonises both. Individual and organisational forms of learning differ, but are closely related to each other. Whilst individual learning is mainly an institutionalised process (courses, seminars), organisational learning occurs incidentally, on a day to day basis.

168. Although the permanent training of active workers has a privileged environment in firms and enterprises, it should not be considered an exclusively private responsibility. Training is in a borderline zone between public and private domains, insofar as it produces a complex output that has the characteristics of a public good, but is also partially or totally appropriated by private individuals and firms.

169. Besides, as new productive models pass from a demand for qualifications to a demand for competencies, the formulation, evaluation and accreditation of such competencies make it necessary to alternate apprenticeship on the job, with theoretical vocational training in educational contexts.

170. The training of active workers, measured in terms of number of participants, is now one of the main items in the activities of vocational training institutions. At night, or early in the morning, the streets of many capital cities of Latin America and the Caribbean witness the massive outflow of workers from training Centres and Units, going to their places of work after two or three hours of daily training. Modalities known as complementary and induction training account for about 70% of the total recruitment of training institutions, which is clear proof of the demand of employed workers to improve their skills and competencies.

The programmes of the **SENA** of **Colombia** for employed workers have been adapted to the specific demands of enterprises, which can now deliver training directly according to approved plans, and get reimbursement for their investment up to 50% of their contribution payable to the training institution.

The **INSAFORP** of **El Salvador** calls for bids for "made to measure" training programmes for enterprises that require skilled workers. Sugar mill and airline workers are trained and upgraded with such programmes.

In **Brazil,** sometimes the needs of highly specialised workers have to be met. For example, in the State of Sao Paulo a Mercedes Benz assembly plant has a SENAI training school attached to it, with a permanent body of trainers and technicians to provide a timely response to the employees' requirements. Recently, the plant was faced with a difficult situation: the sales of vehicles had dropped and there were energy restrictions, so that the production line had to change over to motor generators

171. In **Brazil**, the **SENAI National Technology Centres** (SENAITEC in Spanish), are a model that has two simultaneous assets: creating a system of internal incentives to renew a large organisation with a long institutional history, and to look for new ways of adapting to the qualitative and quantitative demands of its industrial customers. The notion underlying this experience is that a vocational training centre cannot only focus on training, but must incorporate technological innovations to its teaching processes. This subsequently led to a more comprehensive attitude of support and services to enterprises. SENAITEC Centres endeavour to promote a vanguard sort of education, for which it is necessary to know their clients and the market. They also have to enrich and modularise their curricula, including components of every sort; they must organise distance education and task turnover, in order to achieve functional polyvalence.

172. In **Chile,** the **Programa Empresa** includes the majority of trainees in the country. It promotes training at the level of firms and enterprises, and its beneficiaries are the workers in those undertakings. It is therefore a response to demand, financed through a tax incentive (the equivalent of 1% of workers' wages). Some of the structural characteristics of the Programa Empresa are:

• It is financed by the State; its courses must be authorised by the **SENCE** and they are implemented by recognised agencies.
• Firms and enterprises may organise training activities in different ways: they can deliver direct training with their own personnel or with external agents; they can subcontract the courses offered by authorised training bodies **(OTE),** such as universities, professional institutes, technical training centres, or offer training through **Recognised Intermediary Technical Organisations (OTIR).**

The latter (OTIR) were created in1989, owing to the fact that enterprises made little use of the tax franchise and asymmetries were detected between the training offer and the firms' demand. The move was intended to facilitate access to training, creating a scale economy for small and medium sized companies, and providing better information about existing training alternatives. These bodies give technical support to the promotion, organisation and supervision of training programmes. They also provide dissemination, follow-up, quality control and administration services.

173. In **Guatemala,** the **INTECAP** has implemented a straightforward plan that evidences its intent to bring training opportunities within the reach of all workers. The INTECAP centres keep their doors open every day of the week and offer their services from Monday to Saturday on morning, afternoon and evening shifts, and on Sundays in two shifts.

174. In **Mexico,** the **CIMO Programme** is another interesting experience insofar as it is a novel institutional approach organised by the State in the framework of active labour market policies. The State makes it possible for enterprises -especially small and medium sized ones- to have access to a number of resources (technological and managerial know-how, market information, arrangements with financial organisations, workers' training) that can help them in surviving and prospering in the market, and keeping and increasing their personnel. The State does not provide training and counselling to firms with the programme staff, but acts as an intermediary between the offer of services and the demands and needs of enterprises. The programme operates on a decentralised basis through promotional units (UPC) located in all federal states of the country. Each UPC has programme representatives, who are centrally co-ordinated by national consultants, under a department of the Secretariat of Labour and Social Security. The programme is linked to the employers' sector in four different ways:

• The first link is institutional: UPCs are hosted by intermediate corporate organisations, that provide them with a physical space for operation.
• The second link is the demand of training programmes by enterprises.
• The third one, the financial contributions made by companies requesting UPC services.
• The fourth channel is through the offer of services. From 80% to 90% of the business counselling and training contracted, is of private origin.

175. As mentioned earlier, in the **Dominican Republic** the national vocational training institution has recently developed and adopted the so-called Strategic Plan **INFOTEP ACCION 2005.** This Plan was devised to achieve greater coverage and build up a National System of Training for Productive Work. For that purpose its first objective is to bolster up interrelation mechanisms between members of that System. An institutional conception is then envisaged in which INFOTEP will continue to be the dominant body of vocational training in the country, but it will adopt open co-operation strategies with other agents, both public and private. In this manner, and as conveyed by the Plan's second objective, it will expand the System's quantitative and qualitative coverage so as to efficiently meet the demand for occupational training in the country. Two strategies implemented by INFOTEP in this connection are worth citing:

• The identification and promotion of **collaborating centres.** They may be public or private entities that are recognised to proffer vocational training programmes, that they implement under contract with the auspices of INFOTEP, with shared or delegated management. The centres with delegated management carry out the whole training procedure, from information and selection of participants to their certification, with the help and supervision of INFOTEP. Those with

73

shared management deliver the training with an INFOTEP subsidy for administration and use of the infrastructure and equipment.

• The implementation of **dual training,** which has helped in taking training to enterprises. Nowadays there are nearly 30 technical committees made up by employers, workers, specialists and/or experts in given occupational areas, with the following responsibilities: identifying job profiles; taking part in curricular planning, organisation and design; furnishing information about the technological development of job clusters; acting as liaison with various professional associations, and co-operating in the training of instructors. Evaluating committees have also been created to check out the certification process of the training imparted.

• INFOTEP has successfully used a methodology called SIMAPRO to improve productivity from a diagnosis of the skills and competencies that have to be developed to achieve the full performance of workers, give meaning and relevance to training activities, in order to raise the productivity indexes of beneficiary enterprises. The Institute has reported several instances of the successful application of this methodology, that combines training with competitiveness management.

Vocational training for the young

176. The problem of youth unemployment is seen in all the world, even in developed countries, as a high priority social challenge. The young people segment has to face all the obstacles and complications we have been analysing with greater difficulty than the average person: youth unemployment rates double and triplicate general unemployment. This age-group vulnerability is augmented if to short years are added poverty, gender, rural residence and low schooling. The phenomenon is replicated in developed countries.

The significance and priority attained by this issue has led to the creation of a **high level network for the promotion of youth employment policies.** It was a global initiative promoted by the ILO Director General, Juan Somavía, the Secretary General of the United Nations, Kofi Annan, and the President of the World Bank, James Wolfensohn. This joint global initiative was announced by the Secretary General of the United Nations in his report to the Millennium Summit. On that occasion it received the support of Chiefs of State and Government of the whole world who, in the Millennium Declaration, agreed to "develop and apply strategies that may offer young people throughout the world the real possibility of finding dignified and productive work". The network will take advantage of the experience of the leaders in private industry, civil society and economic policy to study innovative approaches and undertake concrete action in order to deal with the difficult problem of youth unemployment.

The employment of young people is a priority area in the ILO decent work programme. At the beginning of the new Century the problem of youth unemployment still persists both in developed and developing countries, and there is a disproportionately large number of young men and women in a situation of long-standing unemployment, or forced to work precariously or with short-term contracts. As a result of this situation, many of them drop out of the labour force, or fail to adapt to their first job, and consequently cease to be active. Socially disfavoured young people are often particularly affected by this condition, and a vicious circle of poverty and social exclusion is thereby perpetuated. In developing countries, where very few can afford to be idle, the problem is rather one of underemployment and ill-remunerated, bad quality jobs in the huge non-structured sector. Consequently, the promotion of productive employment for the young is of special importance for the decent work programme of the ILO. Efforts in that direction are guided by a recognition of the need for effective policies and programmes to raise the standard of living of young persons, and facilitate their full integration into society.

177. The seriousness of the issue and the urgency to find solutions to it are reinforced by current social and demographic data for Latin America and the Caribbean. These point to the persistence of two main features: a high percentage of people under 24 years of age, who today account for 50% of the population; and the conditioning factors of structural poverty, i.e. the extreme segmentation that has been traditional in the Region, and the implementation of structural changes with high unemployment rates. 39% of the inhabitants of Latin America and the Caribbean are below the poverty line.

178. The situation is aggravated by the fact that it is by no means occurring in a context of globalised technical change and productive models, which might reassert a paradigm of lifelong education. In 1999 the open unemployment rate in the Region was much higher than in 1990. Breaking down figures, youth unemployment is from 1.3 to 3.8 times higher than general unemployment.

179. Segmentation of the labour market becomes more marked and discriminating in the case of young manpower, since the educational credentials, skills, aptitudes, attitudinal profile required for access to the modern sector of the economy are almost exclusive of young people of the privileged classes. High-income strata enjoy the benefit of protracted decision, in the sense that they can postpone the advent of full maturity. They may accumulate years of instruction, of vocational search, trial and error, wide socialising experiences, without the pressing need of the poor to get a job -however precarious- at an early age to earn their keep, with the consequent loss of formal education and training opportunities.

180. The sector of excluded young people is made up by the young unemployed with low schooling, inactive young people (who neither study nor work), poor women (mainly adolescent), poor rural inhabitants and members of ethnic minorities. The lack of social networks (family or group networks account for 50% of the labour recruitment of young adolescents) as well as discriminated access to education and quality training is compounded by ecological discrimination (They live in remote areas, with poor communications, scarce and expensive services, which adds to their isolation).

181. In a gender perspective, statistical data show that: 1) the female unemployment rate is 50% higher than that of men; 2) informality is 12% higher among women; 3) female occupations require less skills, have lesser remuneration and safety, and provide an example of double segmentation (horizontal and vertical).

182. If these young people do get a job, it is more precarious, less skilled and worse paid than that of an adult. As getting employment is so difficult, and what is available is of such low quality, a "culture of unstable or non-existent work" grows, that produces inactive young people. The feeling of constant change and uncertainty of modern society also contributes to this paralysis. Being excluded then means economic poverty, low educational credentials, being left out of the social circuit, not being able take part in things, and being deprived of the possibility of becoming a full member of democratic society.

183. Current youth employment policies are defined within those parameters. Some of their main characteristics are as follows:

• In first place, and regarding their rationale, employment and training policies for the young share the central idea and doctrinal basis of the economic model: persons have to be made ready for access into the labour market, rather than protected from its fluctuations.
• Secondly, they are policy tools specifically designed for the young population, or sectors thereof; what in the specialised jargon are known as "focalised" social policies.
• Thirdly, in their most innovative versions they seek for a combination of public and private efforts and resources, to act both upon the labour offer and the demand for employment.
• Fourthly, these new policies and their various programmes represent a change in the role of the State. Briefly, it may be summarised as ascribing a subsidiary part to it, wherefore the State lies aside the direct execution of actions and delegates it to private agents, which remain under its jurisdiction through procedures of bidding and tenders. The State takes on the design and financing of programmes, defines target populations, and evaluation and control mechanisms.

• Fifthly, the State also delegates decisions about the relevance of the various activities, that are generally guided by what are known as "market signals"

184. In **Argentina,** the most characteristic programme of this type is the **"Proyecto Joven",** started in 1993 and conducted by the Secretariat for Employment and Occupational Training of the Ministry of Labour and Social Security. It is financed by the Inter-American Development Bank (IDB) and the National Treasury. The United Nations Development Programme (UNDP) lends it institutional support. The general objective of the project is to improve the possibilities of access into the labour market of young people over 16, from poor homes, by training them for the performance of a regular occupation, and coaching them in the search for employment. Proyecto Joven periodically calls on training institutions to make public bids for the delivery of courses throughout the country. The training offered has to be in keeping with concrete demands of the productive sector. For that reason, the project encourages the joint work of employers and trainers in defining the job profiles required and designing teaching proposals.

Firms and enterprises that host interns make it possible for thousands of young people to have a new labour experience. They are in turn expected to benefit from selecting personnel from among a group of well trained and motivated young candidates. Their lines of action are: a) technical training and internships, and b) providing support in accessing the labour market. The courses of Proyecto Joven are intensive and eminently practical. For its target group, the project establishes 16 years as minimum age, belonging to low-income sectors, an instruction level no higher than complete secondary schooling, and that the young persons should be unemployed or underemployed, with little or no labour experience.

185. The first precedent of programmes of this kind appeared in **Chile** under the title of **Chile Joven.** It was launched in 1991 and is jointly run by the National Training and Employment Service and the Ministry of Labour and Social Security, although some of its schemes are managed by the Social Solidarity and Investment Fund (FOSIS), that depends on the Ministry of Planning. The project's general objective is to improve the chances of access to labour of its beneficiaries, young persons from low-income families, and to help in their social integration (through work or study). Chile Joven has four main lines of action, the first three implemented by SENCE and the fourth one by FOSIS:

• Training and occupational experience at enterprises.
• Alternating Training.
• Enablement for the Creation of Micro-enterprises in the Forestry and Agricultural Sector.
• Occupational Training.

They all combine occupational training with a phase of work experience in plants or enterprises, according to the speciality in question. For the Creation of Micro-enterprises, support to the management of productive undertakings is added.

The target population are young people of low income, preferably between 16 and 24 years of age, (although candidates of up to 30 years are admitted as far as 20% of course participants). They have to be laid off, underemployed, first-time job seekers, with no type of education save night school.

186. Through the **Fondo de Inversión para la Paz,** (Investment Fund for Peace), the Government of Colombia has started implementation of the programme **JÓVENES EN ACCIÓN,** that is part of the "Herramientas para la Paz" package in the context of the "Plan Colombia".

One of the pillars of that strategy is the Social Support Network (RAS) consisting of three programmes for the benefit of populations that are specially vulnerable to the fiscal readjustments and economic recession that the country has gone through in recent years. Those three programmes are **FAMILIAS EN ACCIÓN** (Families in Action), **EMPLEO EN ACCIÓN** (Employment in Action) and **JÓVENES EN ACCIÓN** (Young People in Action). RAS projects are financed with credit granted by the World Bank and the Inter-American Development Bank (IDB).

JÓVENES EN ACCION is aimed at raising employability conditions, and thereby improving the labour and social situation of young people of 18 to 25 years of age, in Fifths 1 and 2 of income distribution in seven main cities in the country (Bogota, Medellin, Cali, Barranquilla, Bucaramanga, Manizales and Cartagena). Planned coverage is of 100,000 young persons over a period of three years, which will make it possible to reach 60% of the target population. Total investment foreseen is U$S 70 million.

Specific objectives of the programme are:

• developing in the young persons the specific skills of a given trade, up to the level of semi-skilled worker;
• promoting the development of basic, social and across-the-board competencies, to improve the candidates' ability to relate to others, and their labour performance;
• building up the private occupational training offer according to the demands of productive sectors and the characteristics and expectations of the young beneficiaries;
• getting the young candidates and the training agencies nearer to the corporate world.

The Programme offers trainees the following services:

• a comprehensive occupational training package;
• a subsidy to cover transportation and snack services; and
• collective insurance for accidents at work and civil responsibility.

Occupational Training services are offered by Training Agencies (ECAP) selected in public tenders. The institutional framework of the Programme combines two criteria: administrative and operational autonomy, to ensure maximum impact and efficiency, and co-ordination with permanent Vocational Training Institutions and local governments.

187. In **Guatemala,** establishing links between civil society and the State is a special challenge in the country's current political and social context. The **PROJOVEN Project -Integral Support for Young People** in Guatemala- is dispensing technical skills training under rather complex general conditions. PROJOVEN is a joint effort by the German Technical Co-operation (GTZ) and the Ministry of Education (MINEDUC). Government bodies, NGOs and municipal organisations take part, as well as youth organisations. The project is intended to improve the access of young people who are in risk situations, to special programmes and offers, in that way promoting their civic participation. The skills development strategy of PROJOVEN operates at three levels:

• At local level, it tries to provide support for young people threatened by social and economic exclusion. The project carries out a number of pilot activities with young persons and systematises the experiences gathered. These include flexible and open training offers for youngsters in marginalised urban zones, as well as innovative approaches for non-formal education and youth expression. The PROJOVEN models have been a basic element for bolstering self-esteem, promoting confidence in personal capacities, self-assertion and overcoming life's difficulties.
• At intermediate level, the project lays stress on upgrading the performance of organisations connected with the youth sector. PROJOVEN supports skills development through counselling and training and the establishment of networks among the different government and non-government actors. In1996 the project initiated a network of public, private and religious organisations which develops models for action and carries out joint activities with young people who live on the streets. This is so far the only forum in the youth sector with representatives of public and private entities, that regularly exchanges concepts and ideas and co-ordinates activities.
• At macro level an effort is made to gain influence and bring about changes in political conditions regarding youth promotion. In that respect, the project proposes to counsel the different ministries concerned (Education, Labour, Health) on

general subject of youth issues. At the same time, PROJOVEN emphasises the launching of a youth policy, both at local and national level. Apart from building networks among the different institutions that work for the young, and forging links between the State and civil society, the project is above all bent on disseminating successful pilot models among politicians, and advising on the development of an innovative youth policy, in accordance with the country's needs.

188. In **Peru**, the **Programa de Capacitación Juvenil, PROJOVEN** (Youth Occupational Training Programme) promoted by the Ministry of Labour and Social Security, is aimed at facilitating access to the formal market for low-income young people, giving them training and a work experience in keeping with the requirements of the productive sector. PROJOVEN is specifically designed to train young persons (men and women) from 16 to 24 years of age, for a maximum period of 3 months. Candidates must meet certain requirements, such as: belonging to poor homes, with scarce economic resources and inadequate levels of training, with or without complete secondary schooling and a maximum of 300 hours' technical training. PROJOVEN is also intended for public or private training bodies like:

- Occupational Education Centres, Colleges with a Technical Option.
- Higher Institutes, Technological Institutes and Non-university Higher Education Institutes.
- Pedagogic Institutes, Non-professional Colleges.
- Foundations, NGOs, non profit Civil Associations.
- Universities, Educational Consortia or any other institution offering training services.

This Programme operates with a large number of firms and enterprises of all sizes and from all sectors, with which it signs Youth Training Agreements. The Programme's operational strategy follows a demand driven scheme in which Training Bodies (ECAP) are responsible for the design of courses, in co-ordination with firms from the productive sector to ensure the relevance of the training.

The Training Bodies' courses are comprised of:
- *A* **Technical Training Phase,** *with an average duration of 3 months, in which young people are trained in semi-skilled trades at an educational institution.*
- *A remunerated* **Occupational Training Phase** *at a private enterprise, in which candidates get a concrete labour experience for a minimum of 3 months.*

The enterprise fully assumes the following conditions:
- payment of an economic reward of no less than the minimum wage and;
- payment of an accident and health insurance, or the direct costs of such contingencies.

189. Implementation of programmes of this type in **Uruguay** started in 1994 with a project called **"Opción Joven"** that was followed in 1996 by **"Projoven"**. Organisations responsible for this programme are the National Youth Institute (INJU), the Ministry of Education and Culture, the National Employment Board, JUNAE (a tripartite advisory body of the National Employment Division, DINAE, in the sphere of the Ministry of Labour and Social Security), and the DINAE itself. Its general objective consists of providing support for young people from low-income households, so that they may improve their skills and employment opportunities.

The programme's lines are:

• Occupational Guidance Workshop: it is intended to reinforce the occupational culture of the young candidates, provide them with information about the labour market and help them to define an educational and work strategy. Gives them elements for job seeking in their first labour experience.
• Technical Training: courses are offered in co-ordination with the demands of firms and enterprises from the sector.
• Supplementary Training: for young persons with greater training needs. It reinforces aspects like reading and writing abilities and arithmetic, as well as personal and social aspects.
• Internships: provide young people with experience in a work post, in accordance with a pre-determined learning plan. At this stage they get a subsistence allowance from enterprises, and support from the training body.
• Support in Access to Labour: a minimum of 9 candidates per course are expected to get formal employment.

The Projoven target population are young persons from 17 to 24 years, from low income homes, without formal employment, incomplete secondary schooling, preferably heads of households. Participation is on an equal basis for men and women, from the capital city or the interior of the country.

190. Among Caribbean countries significant resources were assigned to enhancing employment opportunities for youth.

Most governments in the subregion have implemented specific schemes and measures targeted at young persons, including apprenticeships, subsidized training and job placements and entrepreneurial development programmes which aim at facilitating their absorption into the labour market in either wage employment or self-employment. Examples of such programmes include the Youth Training and Employment Partnership Programme **(YTEPP)** in Trinidad and Tobago and those run by the Human Employment and Training Trust **(HEART)** in Jamaica. Some countries make provision for start-up capital for those interested in self-employment options. Examples include the **Self-Start Fund** in **Jamaica,** the **Barbados Business Enterprise Fund** and the **Belize Youth Enterprise Fund.**

In the case of **Barbados,** eight(8) major YTEPPs were identified, with the Barbados Government being overwhelmingly the most important actor here. The two most significant programmes, and the two oldest, are managed by the **Barbados Vocational Training Board:** The **National Apprenticeship Programme** and the **Skills Training Programme**. The first programme targets unskilled, unemployed youth and the entry age is 16 years. The Skills Training Programme targets the 16-24 age group and seeks to provide employable skills within the shortest possible time. Two recently started programmes in Barbados are the National Youth Service, which began in 1991, and the Youth Entrepreneurship Scheme initiated in 1995.

In the case of **Jamaica,** one institution -**HEART/NTA-** as the National Training Agency, dominates youth employment training in two senses. First, HEART/NTA is a major provider of training programmes itself. Secondly, many other youth employment training programmes in Jamaica utilize the curricula of this organization and/or also get some form of financial assistance.

One of the most well known programmes conducted by HEART/NTA for the training and employment of youth is the **"School-Leavers Training Opportunities Programme" (SL-TOP).**

The SL-TOP Programme was conceptualised in response to rising unemployment among youth with a secondary education certificate. The programme was conceived as both a job experience and a job training programme at the same time. The skill areas that are offered by the SL-TOP Programme have not been formally defined: the training concentrates on specific functions and jobs in about 35 distinct areas, mostly within the commercial and administrative sectors, rather than on a typified occupation which was supposed to make it fairly flexible. It is noteworthy that participation in SL-TOP is about 73% female, and that the actual enrolment of 4121 trainees in the fiscal year 1998/99 exceeded the projected enrolment of 3,800. The majority of SL-TOP trainees (70%) is placed in companies, with 1,093 companies having participated in the SL-TOP Programme in the same reference period.

The participants in the SL-TOP Programme must be between 17 and 23 years of age and possess at least two general education proficiency certificates. The training programmes take place exclusively on the job and last between 1 and 3 years. In contrast to an apprenticeship, SL-TOP graduates only recently began to attain a certification based on the NVQ-J system, though they are generally better educated than apprentices.

In the case of Trinidad and Tobago, six main YTEPPs can be identified. Five are run by the Government. The largest is the Youth Training and Employment Partnership Programme (YTEPP) which began in 1988. Alongside this, we can identify SERVOL, which is an NGO-based programme initiated in 1970. The former in funded by the World Bank (65%) and the Government, while the latter is financed from grant assistance.

A range of other non-governmental organizations, particularly church-based groups have had a much longer and consistent involvement in youth programmes. However, these NGO efforts have not had a substantial impact in terms of numbers of youth involved, given limited resources and other constraints. One possible exception is the SERVOL organization in Trinidad and Tobago, which has grown from a modest intake of 25 trainees in 1972 to become a major institution of training, particularly for those on the fringes, if not actually, youth at risk.

Vocational training as an instrument for overcoming gender inequalities in the world of labour

191. The radical transformations in the realm of employment and in the generation of knowledge hat marked the end of the 20th Century have caused a redefinition of the very concept of training, its objectives and approaches. This has logically had an effect on gender policies and strategies in training. It sounds a special warning about the sustainability of training actions and how to invest them with the necessary institutional backing to give them continuity. Old models of knowledge generation are being questioned, as well as the social structure, makeup of corporations, economic and social development and production systems; gender relations and representation are being mainstreamed. These paradigms impinge upon, and modify one another, giving rise to a redefinition of the concepts of development, welfare and incorporation of the different social groups and actors. Likewise, a substantial change is taking place in the nature and organisation of cultural values, and in the sexual division of labour, and the irreversibility of female participation. Women:

• are no longer a supplementary labour force. There can be no doubts as to their will to be trained, their educational levels have risen notoriously and they take part in skills development, upgrading and retraining activities more assiduously than men;
• they have consolidated the "dual presence" model, by reconciling labour cycles and family life. Employment has become a determining component of women's life project, their self-assertion and social revaluation. Their right to work is a substantial aspect of their human rights, because the work they perform enables them not only to earn their keep, but to achieve self-realisation and autonomy.

192. Nevertheless, inequalities and discrimination continue, showing that, in truth, women and men do not compete for the same market but have distinct requirements regarding labour supply and demand. A few and diverse reminders can be quoted in this connection:

• Higher unemployment rates and degree of informality. "Female" occupations are concentrated in the lower strata of the labour market in terms of remuneration, qualification, work conditions, social recognition and development prospects.
• Lower wages for equal work; differences get steeper in the more skilled jobs. Significantly higher schooling required for having access to the same employment opportunities as men. In addition, entry into "traditionally male" sectors of technological innovation, or into a position signifying occupational competition, renders resistance and/or hostility more acute.
• Women entrepreneurs set up smaller companies or shops in the less unfolded sectors. Their access to credit is more complex and limited, their availability of information and business opportunities also more restricted.
• The sexual division of labour is the main reason why women are associated with poverty, Their greater likelihood of lapsing into indigence has to do with their social disadvantages for access to and control of productive resources, with their lesser participation in institutions, and the diminished social value of female activities and abilities. Consequently, they have greater difficulties for getting into the market and staying there.
• The gender distribution of labour makes women responsible for personal care tasks, most of them unremunerated. These are activities of extremely high social worth, on which the development of future generations depends. However, the market penalises such services by not including them in national accounts, and ascribing them to public offer.
• The remarkable development of Information and Communications Technologies (ICTs) is creating a new gender gap: the digital divide. According to the Human Development Report (UNDP 1999), the typical user of the Internet, at world scale, is male, under 35, has a university education and high income, lives in an urban area and speaks English. The tendency starts early on in life: in the U.S.A. five more boys than girls use computers at home, and parents spend twice as much on technology products for their sons than for their daughters.

193. Hence the need, and the possibility, of generating active policies with a gender perspective from vocational training institutions. This implies making sure that the specific needs of women and men are contemplated in an overall manner. The right of women to training has to be considered a fundamental human right; in developing and enhancing their capacities it becomes a tool to promote and strengthen their employability and access to labour. Likewise, women have to be offered full social, economic and political participation, in compliance with the democratic principle of gender equality, and to combat poverty. With this conviction, it is

possible to take action to modify individual and collective situations regarding female labour, in order to attain a more integrating and less imperfect model vis-à-vis decent work. Modifying individual situations implies not only upgrading female competencies for employability, diversifying women's options and facilitating their access to training with real occupational possibilities, but also bolstering their self-esteem and helping them to identify and overcome the obstacles and stereotypes that surround them. Transforming the culture of a society means promoting a change of cultural and corporate patterns to confer a new social and economic value upon female qualities and singularities. It implies favouring the shared responsibility of society as a whole, public and private organisations, men and women, regarding care and attention tasks. It also entails making alliances to include systematic consideration of the situation of working women, their training and gender relations at work, etc., in collective bargaining, trade union activities and the human resources policies of enterprises. In sum, the promotion (through training) of comprehensive, across-the-board policies that may operate at all levels where there is gender discrimination; the stimulation of synergies among the various agents to build up a framework in which the different organisations may contribute with their own characteristics and mandates, and have a multiplier effect.

194. This conception -that of course, is not generalised- characterises some innovations towards the end of the 20th Century in Latin America. Different "action models" can be identified, with various degrees of complexity in design and scope. They may be models aimed exclusively at women, or of a mixed nature with a gender slant. They may be public or private, addressed to specific groups within the female population, or intended to expand women's participation, but they all have the common denominator of resorting to comprehensive intervention as the most appropriate way to bring about equal opportunities at work and in training. They consequently contribute to the attainment of decent work by all women and men.

195. Some of these models are illustrated below. A single case is described for each one, by way of example.

 • *Training Programmes in co-ordination with national policies to promote equal opportunities.*

A)   Aimed specifically at women.
Occupational Training Programme for Women Heads of Households (PMJH in Spanish), Chile (under way since 1992).

Co-ordinated by SERNAM (National Women's Service), implemented by municipalities, with the participation of various State institutions, SENCE among them. Its general objective is to improve the economic situation of women in charge of their household, raise their standard of living and that of their family members and stamp out any kind of discrimination.

Main lines of action are: Occupational Training (Municipal Team); Training and Placement in Salaried Work (SENCE); Support to Independent Labour (FOSIS); Supplement in Basic and Secondary Education (MINEDUC, Municipalities); Access to Health Services, Child Care and Legal Assistance. The Programme management and methodology lay stress on: integrity, twofold focus, participation and decentralisation (centralised design, local implementation, co-ordination of public and private resources at local, regional and national level).

B) With a gender slant
Plano Nacional de Qualificação do Trabalhador (PLANFOR), Brazil (under way since 1996)
Implemented by the National Secretariat of Occupational Training and Development (SEFOR) of the Ministry of Labour, with resources supplied by the Fund for the Protection of Workers (FAT), and managed by a tripartite Deliberating Council of equal participation.

Its specific objectives include: "combating all forms of discrimination, especially in connection with gender, age, race and colour, in order to ensure respect for diversity". To implement this, gender is to be incorporated as a category and will serve as a working tool for the planning and delivery of vocational training programmes promoting equality of the sexes. Innovative experiences have proliferated, especially in the revaluation of niches for the generation of work and earnings, that in turn improve the quality of the family and community life of low-income populations.

• *Training Programmes promoted by the actors themselves, with the support of international co-operation*

A)   Aimed specifically at women
Programa Mujeres Adolescentes de Centro América (Central American Adolescent Women's Programme) (European Union and Social Integration Council (CIS) (1997-1998)
The CIS was official regional representative, in order to guarantee the political impact of activities. Each country appointed a national body in charge, that acted as national counterpart: in **Costa Rica**, it was the **National Centre for Women and the Family**; in **Nicaragua**, the **National Women's Institute**, and in **Honduras**, the **National Welfare Board**. Many other government and non-government organisations took part in the implementation of activities.

There were two priority lines of action: prevention of social risks and technical training of women teenagers. Methodological choices were: strengthening of civil society, development of public policies, implementation of multiple complementary activities in communities, reinforcement of local agents and powers. Emphasis was also laid on synergy and interconnection among sub-projects The problems of female adolescents were approached from various points of view: the gender perspective, compliance with human rights and building up emergent citizenship. Awareness was promoted among the young women, which will enable them to value their own image. They were also urged to see to those around them.

The autonomy and creativity of participating organisations was duly taken into account.

B) With a gender slant
Proyecto Comayagua de Educación para el Trabajo (Comayagua Project of Ocupational Education -POCET), Honduras (under way since 1990)

Implemented by the National Vocational Training Institute (INFOP) and the Secretariat for Public Education. It has received international assistance from the ILO, the UNDP and the Netherlands Government. Its target group were the inhabitants of rural and semi-urban communities, between 15 and 49 years of age; an explicit effort was made to reach women. It dealt with the need to establish closer links between formal and informal education and labour, creating internal complementary mechanisms.

The POCET training approach endeavours to bring together literacy and elementary education components with occupational training ones. It also tries to turn educational processes into productive work, by carrying out concrete activities, and setting up self-managed communal or inter-community production associations. The purpose is to contribute to the development of a new culture of relations between men and women, based on a revaluation and redistribution of tasks, and to improve women's access to sustainable productive activities. A gender perspective was incorporated at different levels of the programme, with a specific component, "Education, Labour and Women", devoted to the design of strategies and instruments, and to vocational training.

In the communal area, it included: a) measures to facilitate women's participation, such as courses at convenient times and places, and child care services; b) promoting awareness among men; c) bolstering of women's self-esteem and their capacity to act in public, etc.; and d) positive discrimination measures to have access to credit, etc.

C) Including at the same time the mainstreaming of the gender perspective, and specific action
Programa de Fortalecimiento de la Formación Técnica y Profesional de Mujeres de Bajos Ingresos -FORMUJER- (Programme for Strengtening the

Technical and Vocational Training of Low-income Women) (under way since 1998)

Project co-financed by the Inter-American Development Bank (IDB). Cinterfor/ILO is in charge of regional co-ordination and technical supervision. National Pilot Projects are the responsibility of the Ministry of Labour, Employment and Development of Human Resources in Argentina; INFOCAL in Bolivia and INA in Costa Rica. It has two objectives: building up the quality, relevance and gender equity of technical-vocational education in the Region, and transferring and disseminating the models and methodologies evolved, and the lessons learned. It endeavours to act simultaneously, in a co-ordinated manner, on the logic of mainstreaming the gender perspective, and on specific measures and focalised activities for groups of women in unfavourable conditions, in order to expand and diversify female participation. To give its objectives sustainability and institutionality, the project deals with the gender perspective as one more aspect of innovative processes in the design and management of vocational training. For that purpose, it develops a broad methodological package built around improving the employability of persons. It also promotes social dialogue by means of alliances with numerous actors, aimed at inducing a change in social and entrepreneurial culture that may favour the access of women to labour.

For more details see: Cinterfor/ILO Report 1999/2000, or the site Mujer, Formación y Trabajo (Women, Training and Labour) of the Cinterfor/ILO web page (www.cinterfor.org.uy).

V
VOCATIONAL TRAINING AS A SPACE FOR SOCIAL DIALOGUE AND A TOOL FOR PROMOTING IT

196. Social dialogue is the oldest and most permanent precept of ILO action in all the world. It is also, perhaps, the one that lies closest to the Organisation's essence and mission. In effect, the tripartite approach -that is at the same an ILO structural principle and a programme line- presupposes the existence of fluent social dialogue. Today, on the threshold of a new Century, it is still urgent and necessary to have strong and active social and government actors, as well as opportunities for dialogue that may show the way for economic and social development, with due consideration of the various social interests. Creation of the InFocus Technical Programme with that precise objective in view, ratifies the essential need to lend support to actors for engaging in social dialogue.

Vocational training as a meeting point of different interests and actors

197. There are at present serious difficulties in Latin America and the Caribbean to bring social dialogue to the fore. The situation faced by national governments on the whole gives them little leeway for independent decision, in view of the conditions imposed by the new contexts of trade opening, international competition and financial globalisation. Within governmental structures, labour ministries often have to deal with the consequences of decisions and processes adopted outside their sphere, and sometimes are not convened to discuss the economic agenda. This occurs at the same time as the type and scope of the demands placed upon them multiplies and increases.

198. The various social actors, for their part, also face situations of relative weakness. Employers' organisations usually fail to go beyond purely reactive strategies vis-à-vis the changes caused by openness and globalisation. The growth of small and micro-enterprises, as well as that of the informal sector of the economy, undermine their capacity to organise and represent the productive endeavours of the countries. Affiliated enterprises, in turn, demand that these organisations diversify their services to include the technological area, commercial counselling, training, etc.

199. The case of workers' organisations is even more complex. The disappearance of permanent employment patterns, the shrinking of industrial, formal, wage-earning jobs, pose difficult challenges for trade unions that have to represent the interests of men and women workers in extremely diverse labour situations, that differ increasingly from those that prevailed when the labour movement was born and flourished. Most workers' organisations have not managed to adapt conceptually and operationally to a reality in which there is a massive number of informal labourers and unemployed workers, where the labour force is partly feminised, and large contingents of young people try to enter the labour market. If employers' organisations have lost their lobbying power to have an effect, for instance, on the countries' tariffs policies, workers' unions have lost ground in bargaining for wages, work stability and legislation to protect their rights.

200. For the above reasons (and others), creating spaces and opportunities for social dialogue, and making them last, has more often than not been an arduous task in Latin America and the Caribbean. However, within this general picture there is a field where dialogue and agreement seem feasible: vocational training.

201. Simultaneously, **training has ceased to be a secondary topic in labour relations, and has shifted to a more prominent position.** To a degree, this is due to the growing importance of the knowledge factor in production and work processes, and to the fact that training has come to be considered a key element in strategies to raise productivity and improve competitiveness. But it is also the result of more equitable conditions in the access to education and employment opportunities.

202. Although the social actors have lost negotiating clout in other areas, in vocational training they appear to be potentially strong. Through their class organisations, both employers and workers are playing an increasingly active role in the life of vocational training institutions (or demand to do so). They are creating their own training agencies, sometimes with bipartite management, and by mutual agreement have incorporated training into collective bargaining.

203. Ministries of Labour, for their part, are no longer exclusively devoted to mediation in conflicts between capital and labour, and have assumed a leading part on the training scene. At present, there is not a single Ministry of Labour in the Region that does not have a training service or unit. In some countries, Labour Ministries are formally in charge of laying down policies and managing funds for training. Together with this repositioning of Ministries of Labour and social agents in the sphere of vocational training, novel experiences of social dialogue have emerged, both at national and local and sectoral level.

204. Such occurrences show, in the first place, that vocational training is a field where the different actors are normally more likely to reach agreement. In fact, many of the above-mentioned spaces have fared well in contexts that were highly conflictive for other reasons. Secondly, the possibility of concluding agreements and attaining results in this area enables the actors to "learn", i.e. discussions about vocational training can teach the actors to discuss, and reach agreement about other subjects that had proved too conflictive and difficult. This is not such a naive notion as it might seem. The truth is that adequately approached, vocational training is never an aseptic topic, separate from the other subjects involved in labour relations, such as employment, wages, working conditions, occupational safety and hygiene, productivity, quality, etc. It is closely connected to all of them. The difference is that it is easier to agree about it, and for that reason it is a good beginning for social dialogue experiences.

205. Existing experiences, however, have the weak points of incipient things. Employers' and workers'organisations do not have enough delegates adequately prepared to act in spaces for social dialogue on vocational training. Knowledge about international experiences is still scarce. It might be very useful for Andean and Central American countries to get acquainted with the relatively greater achievement of their Southern Cone neighbours, and with what has been done in the European Union. The broadening of services of employers' and workers' organisations to embrace vocational training is bringing them many benefits, but also causing many difficulties and discussions as to how far they should become involved, for instance, in the implementation of public training and employment policies.

Spaces for social dialogue on vocational training

206. Precedents of vocational training serving as an area for social dialogue in Latin America and the Caribbean go as far back as the very origins of national training bodies. This is, precisely, one of the distinctive features of training in the Region since many of those institutions adopted tripartite or multipartite forms of management. This characteristic is still continued in several countries, and in a few of them it has become more marked through subregional and sectoral decentralisation processes. Such are the cases of INA in Costa Rica, SENA in Colombia, INFOTEP in the Dominican Republic, INAFORP in Panama, or INCE in Venezzuela, among others.

207. More recently, however, a diversity of areas and spaces for social dialogue have been created in the Region, in which vocational training is the central theme of debate and negotiation. Promotion of social dialogue around training is based on the understanding that it is an indispensable element to reach the objective of

adequate and relevant training action vis-à-vis the productive apparatus of countries (or regions therein), as well as a necessary precondition for the social endorsement of training policies. It also causes the actors in the realm of labour to get effectively involved in the development and implementation of the various vocational training activities.

208. Apart from the already mentioned example of national vocational training institutions, it is now possible to single out different levels at which social dialogue on training is going on. In the first place there are public, tripartite bodies in charge of planning, managing and monitoring training policies at national level. In Latin America and the Caribbean there are numerous instances of such organisations, such as:

• The **Consejo Deliberativo del Fundo de Amparo ao Trabalhador, CODEFAT** (Deliberating Council of the Fund for the Protection of Workers), **Brazil.** This is a tripartite body that manages the FAT, built up with the contributions both of workers and employers of the formal sector of the economy. Part of the FAT fund goes to financing the activities of the national employment system, like unemployment insurance, careers guidance and placement, vocational training programmes for different groups, jobs and income generation projects, etc.

• In **Chile**, a **Consejo Nacional de Capacitación** (National Training Council) was created as a result of the restructuring of the SENCE in 1997. The Council has at tripartite structure (but no equal participation) and its function is to advise the Ministry of Labour on the formulation of a national training policy. It was set up for counselling purposes, and therefore has no resolving power.

• In **Mexico**, the **CONOCER**, is a tripartite entity whose tasks are planning, implementing, promoting and updating a Standardised System for the Certification of Occupational Competencies. The CONOCER scheme includes the phases of identification and standardisation of competencies, training and certification, wherefore it covers all aspects of the concept of labour competency. In the design of the Standardised System for the Certification of Occupational Competencies, a very important role is played by the Standardisation Committees, made up by workers and employers who usually represent a branch of activity. With he technical support of CONOCER, these Committees identify skills and competencies and turn them into standards.

• In **Uruguay,** the **Junta Nacional de Empleo, JUNAE** (National Employment Board), a tripartite organisation in the sphere of the Ministry of Labour and Social Security, is in charge of managing a Fund for Occupational Retraining. This fund is made up by contributions both from workers and employers, and is used to finance retraining courses for workers on unemployment insurance, as well as training courses for particularly disfavoured social groups in the labour market.

Secondly, there are the tripartite public entities in charge of planning and managing training policies at regional or local level. Just as incorporating the partners of the labour relationship has been deemed indispensable to adapt training actions, and make them relevant to the needs of productive mechanisms, decentralisation and democratisation of the training demand has always been a precondition for bringing the training requirements of workers and productive units as near as possible to the offer of the many agents that deliver training. The following can be mentioned among experiences of social dialogue on training at regional or local scale:

• In **Brazil,** the **Comisiones Estaduales y Municipales de Empleo** (State and Municipal Employment Committees). They have been set up as an instrument to decentralise and democratise the activities financed through the FAT fund. They are tripartite bodies one of whose main functions is to assess requests for credit for training activities at the level of federal states and municipalities.

• In **Chile,** the **Consejos Regionales de Capacitación** (Regional Training Councils) have been created, regional tripartite bodies of regional scope, that advise regional governments about implementation of national training policies at local level.

• Although not developed within public organisations, the **Consejos de Capacitación y Formación Profesional** (Vocational Education and Training Councils) currently operating in the cities of Rosario, Mendoza and Comodoro Rivadavia, Argentina, are an interesting case of social dialogue on training at regional level. These councils are bipartite, made up by workers' and employers' organisations, and were created to upgrade the occupational profiles of active and circumstantially unemployed workers in the different Provinces and regions.

In the third place, there are instances of bipartite negotiation and dialogue, by workers' and employers' organisations, that may occur by branch of activity or at the level of individual enterprises. We may point out here that actual collective agreements (either by branch of activity or enterprise) will be dealt with in the next section, specifically devoted to collective bargaining on training, which is no doubt another form of social dialogue. The following examples of bipartite social dialogue on training can be quoted:

• In **Argentina,** the **Consejos de Capacitación y Formación Profesional** (Vocational Education and Training Councils) apart from being regional -reason for which they were included in the previous section- are also an instance of bipartite social dialogue and therefore cited here as well.

• **Comités Bipartitos de Capacitación** (Bipartite Training Committees), in **Chile**. They have been set up at the level of enterprises in order to agree about, and evaluate training programmes for workers, and provide counselling on training to the enterprises' management. A Committee of this type must be set up in all firms employing 15 or more workers. The cost of training activities carried out by enterprises with the endorsement of Bipartite Committees, will be deductible from corporate taxes up to 1% of the respective company's payroll.

• In **Uruguay**, the **Fundación para la Capacitación de trabajadores y empresarios de la Industria de la Construcción** (Training Foundation for Workers and Employers of the Construction Industry). This Foundation resulted from a Collective Agreement signed by workers and employers in 1997. It is charged with managing the vocational training, qualification and occupational certification of workers and employers in the sector. It also carries out studies and research that may contribute to raise the sector's competitiveness, and keep up employment levels in it.

Fourthly, a number of major changes have taken place over the past few years to challenge vocational training institutions in the Caribbean. The results have led to a more proactive **TVET** system which is being reflected at both national and regional levels in vocational skill delivery, skill qualification recognition, and the promotion of greater institutional linkages. The participation of employers and workers organizations, jointly with national governments, became one of the most significant issues. The current institutionality includes a new way of social actors involvement in the design and operation of vocational training policies and programmes; besides, it has a meaningful impact on the development of National Vocational Qualifications bodies where employers, workers and governments are also concerned.

Among these changes the following can be mentioned: removing of vocational training provision from the public to the private sector; lower offer of non-specialised low-income jobs; strengthening of human resources development policies which motivates people to self-development; and, the trend of **CARICOM** towards a unique economy. These trends are not only redefining the labour environment, but they are also modifying the way in which people prepare themselves for work.

The impetus behind the changes in the operation of technical vocational education and training (TVET) institutions is part of a broadening strategic vision in areas related to employment-driven training. Such a vision is being articulated in the way people seek meaningful work through support from TVET institutions. The view in the region suggests that jobs need to offer both economic rewards and life fulfillment, through self-expression and dignity.

In particular, this influence is being shaped by major organizational activities reflected in the development of TVET coordinating units, i.e. **National Training Agency (NTA).** Such Governmental organizations at the national level are created with a purpose of narrowing the skill gap by promoting a seamless educational infrastructure in collaboration with trade unions and employers' organizations. Such agencies are represented in the Caribbean by the HEART **Trust/NTA** in **Jamaica,** the **National Training Agency in Trinidad and Tobago,** the **Technical Vocational Education and Training Council** in **Barbados,** and the recently created **Guyana Training Agency.** The establishment of a similar NTA type agency is also under discussion in **Saint Lucia.**

The need to articulate labour market information and vocational requirements at the national and regional level has not been lost in the work carried out by many TVET agencies in the Caribbean region. One action in particular that has been gaining prominence in bringing together Government, employers, and trade union to articulate more accurately the skill job match has been through the development of common vocational qualifications, a process that TVET agencies in the Caribbean are conscientiously pursuing.

In addition to the formulation of NTAs in Jamaica, Barbados, Trinidad y Tobago y Guyana, the agencies are in the process of developing a competent workforce through establishing national vocational qualifications that are competency-based. Developed through tripartite initiatives, competency-based vocational qualifications are benchmarked internationally to ensure the end product meets the performance requirements of industry. The NTAs are also collaborating to formally recognize each other's national skill competencies/qualifications and have entered into discussions on formulating at some point a regional Caribbean Vocational Qualification (CVQ). Together, these innovative initiatives have anticipated the current discussion by CARICOM member states regarding the free movement of skills and the implementation of Protocol II, while focusing on common vocational standards and accreditation.

Collective bargaining and vocational training

209. Vocational training is an increasingly important element in collective bargaining, in its different forms and levels. As from the moment that training started to play a part in the labour relations' scheme, it was inevitable that it should sooner or later be included in collective bargaining. In effect, as a right of workers, training is liable to be provided for in collective agreements as one more labour entitlement. As it is also an economic instrument, employers may be very much interested in regulating it through negotiation. On the other hand, collective agreements are flexible devices, capable of adapting to training needs that vary according to incessant technological changes. Finally, at various bargaining levels (enterprises, branches of activity, national or even international level) there is a wide range of alternatives that may be more or less suitable for different aspects of vocational training. For example, comprehensive framework agreements or national social

pacts are particularly appropriate to lay down broad lines of training policy, and regulate rights and obligations for whole sectors. Collective agreements at the level of enterprises, for their part, can determine the specific training plans of a given firm, and adapt the training provisions of more general agreements and pacts.

210. Although policies of social agreement through national framework arrangements, or social pacts, have been the norm mainly in Europe (especially in Spain and Italy), it is also possible to come across some interesting experiences in Latin America.

Such is the case of **Argentina,** where in the past ten years two social pacts were concluded that had express provisions on vocational training matters. The Framework Agreement on Employment, Productivity and Social Equity, of 1994, includes an important chapter on vocational training that, apart from underlining the importance of training, foresees the drafting of a five-year plan and a national training agreement. It furthermore entrusts to the Labour Ministry the implementation of training programmes agreed upon by the social actors. On the other hand, the Act of Coincidences signed in 1997 by the Government and the General Labour Confederation (employers did not participate), postulated the furtherance of ongoing vocational training and training for the unemployed, as well as participation of the social actors therein. Both pacts (the first one tripartite, the second bipartite) were more conceptual than practical regarding training, and were not implemented to a great extent. Nevertheless, they did advance the critical importance of vocational training in labour policies and relations.

In **Mexico** there are also several social pacts or agreements, some of which make reference to vocational training. One of them, the National Agreement for the Promotion of Quality and Productivity, of 1990, included an innovative provision that was subsequently adopted by other countries: promoting the grouping together of small enterprises to implement joint training programmes at adequate scale.

Similar examples are to be found in Colombia and Panama, among other countries.

211. As opposed to what happens in Europe, centralised collective bargaining by branch of activity is not very frequent in Latin America. It only prevails in Argentina, Brazil and Uruguay, although in all three countries there has been a strong decentralising tendency in recent years. For that reason, it is difficult to find collective agreements by branch of economic activity that include significant training clauses. Exceptions are the collective agreements of the construction industry in

Argentina and Uruguay, that set up training bodies for the sector managed by the social actors.

212. Some large enterprises have collective agreements on vocational training. Sometimes the legislation in force or some State organisation foster negotiation on the matter. Such is the case of Argentine law, that requires that collective agreements should include training clauses, or the Fund for the Protection of Workers in Brazil, or the Labour Retraining Fund in Uruguay, whose resources are available for projects negotiated collectively (although not exclusively).

213. Collective agreements that incorporate training usually have the following type of provision: general programme pronouncements; clauses on free time for training; provisions about special training programmes; creation of bipartite committees for managing those programmes; clauses on the financing of training activities. To a lesser extent, they also refer to incentives to attend courses, scholarships, the employers' duty to offer training, and links between training programmes and personnel redundancy cuts for economic reasons.

214. Worthy of special mention is the first regional (extra national) collective agreement in the Mercosur. It was concluded by the Volkswagen companies of Argentina and Brazil with their respective branch trade unions, in 1999. The arrangement contains an important provision on a "vocational training system", that comprises harmonisation of the training programmes to be developed by the companies' various units; a principle whereby the coaching, courses and seminars of those programmes should be automatically recognised by both companies; and co-operation of the trade unions in the elaboration of the programmes.

215. It can be said that vocational training has started to form part of the contents of collective bargaining in the countries of the Region. The development of collective bargaining with a training ingredient has been uneven, but appears to be promising n some countries.

VI
CONCLUSIONS

216. Decent work is a concept with a profound ethical content, tending to enhance the importance of the rights of workers and the quality of working conditions. Decent work can only be work in sufficient, appropriate, dignified and fair quantity and quality. This includes respect for workers' rights, earnings, satisfactory working conditions and social protection, in a context of trade union freedom and social dialogue.

On the other hand, if training is one of the human rights and also a fundamental requirement for access to employment of good quality – an aspect that becomes more critical in a context of globalisation, regionalisation, predominance of technology and the advent of the so-called society of knowledge – training must needs be an essential part of decent work.

Consequently, nowadays no decent work is possible without adequate training. In the same way as the latter is a precondition and a component of the former, decent work is also an environment that favours ongoing training, updating and retraining.

217. This dynamics of training and decent work has a special dimension to it that has not been specifically developed in this document, but has been referred to in some parts of it, and must be dwelt upon. It is the globalisation and regionalisation that has just been mentioned.[62] The Resolution of the International Labour Conference 2000 on Human Rights also concurs in para. 2, where it says that "it is increasingly acknowledged that globalisation has a social dimension calling for a social answer", and that "education and training are components in an economic and social response to gobalisation".

So that, for instance, both the European Union and the Mercosur, each in its own way and to the extent of their possibilities, have considered the subject of training to be essential, and continue to do so[63].

---

[62] As underlined by SEN, Amartya, *loc.cit.* pp. 138.139
[63] See ERMIDA URIARTE, Oscar and BARRETTO GHIONE, Hugo (co-ord.), *Formación profesional en la integración regional,* Cinterfor/ILO, Montevideo 2000.

99

There is still one final caution. If there is no sufficient and decent work in all the world, the more developed countries will see their problems of unwanted immigration grow indefinitely. And that without going into the theoretical assumption that globalisation of the economy should imply globalisation of the labour force.

218. If we accept that vocational training is part of the notion of decent work, that it is a precondition for the attainment thereof, and furthermore that decent work presupposes access to training, we must agree to the methodological conclusion that some training indicators have to be included in the measurement of decent work.

It will be necessary to measure literacy, schooling and initial training rates. Also it will be necessary to measure the frecuency and extension of continuous training and of the specific training programmes for groups like unemployed, women, young people, etc.. It will also be recommended to quantify the degree in which training is rule by collective bargaining and the level of social actors' participation in their management.

219. Vocational training has a prominent role to play in connection with the ILO strategic objective of creating greater opportunities for women and men to have decorous jobs and earnings. Through co-ordination with information and careers' guidance systems, vocational training may help to bring down unemployment by establishing efficient connections between labour supply and demand. Through a systematic technological updating of its methodologies and contents, vocational training contributes to bridge the gap between the competencies' structure required by the labour market, and that offered by training institutions and systems. Although vocational training is not of itself a direct source of employment generation – except for the jobs required to operate it – it does play a central role in strategies to increase productivity and improve competitiveness in systemic terms. Hence that, although not sufficient, it is absolutely essential for boosting the competitiveness of enterprises, productive sectors and national, regional or local economies, helping to bring about better conditions for employment generation. Vocational training is besides the main tool for improving the employability of working women and men. It is a personal task, but also entails responsibility for society at large and the agents involved. In this respect, the countries of Latin America and the Caribbean have been making considerable progress in the development of lifelong training and education systems, dealing not only with their heterogeneous demand for qualifications, but also the changing training demands of people in the course of their lives.

220. The ILO strategic objective of enhancing the scope and efficiency of social protection for all, also has in vocational training a fundamental tool for its accomplishment. Regardless of the efforts that may be made to improve the coverage and effectiveness of social security systems, it is every day more evident that

equitably distributed opportunities for training are an essential part of the current menu of social protection policies. Promoting equal opportunities necessarily leads to training strategies specifically designed and implemented to counteract the situations of inequity and vulnerability suffered by certain groups. Such is the case of unemployed workers, active workers facing technological recycling processes or precarious employment, young people and women.

221. Anyway, going back now to the conceptual realm, it is quite clear that in the current framework in which education and labour tend to converge[64] "education and training are the cornerstone for a decent job" [65].

222. Vocational training is a particularly fertile ground for the development and strengthening of social dialogue. In comparison with other subjects, traditionally more controversial, the approach of the diverse interests and positions result more feasible, depending on its contribution to objectives such as the improvement of productivity and competitiveness, but also and simultaneously to the social integration and inclusion and to the personal and professional development of female and male workers. The Latin American and the Caribbean experience confirms this statement, considering the appearance of different and multiples negotiation, settlement and dialogue experiences on vocational training. The latter also maintains important links with other subjects of the labour relation systems, which on one hand marks it as an indisputable component of these, and on the other hand, places it as a possible starting point for a positively directed negotiation between employers, workers and government in the most diverse fields.

[64] "Learning and working become related pursuits" ILO *Globalizing Europe*....cit. p.1.
[65] ILO, *Resolution....cit.* para. 3.

ACRONYMS USED

AENOR — Asociación Española de Normalización y Certificación

CARICOM	Caribbean Community
CBT	Community Based Training
CETP/UTU	Consejo de Educación Técnico Profesional - Universidad del Trabajo, Uruguay
CIMO	Programa de Calidad Integral y Modernización, Mexico
CINTERFOR	Inter-American Research and Documentation Centre on Vocational Training
CODEFAT	Conselho Deliberativo do Fundo do Amparo ao Trabalhador, Brasil
CONET	Consejo Nacional de Educación Técnica, Argentina
CONOCER	Consejo de Normalización y Certificación de Competencia Laboral, Mexico
CUT	Central Única dos Trabalhadores, Brazil
CVQ	Caribbean Vocational Qualification

DINAE	Dirección Nacional de Empleo, Uruguay
DGCC	Dirección General de Centros de Capacitación, Mexico

FAT	Fundo do Amparo ao Trabalhador, Brazil
FIP	Fondo de Inversión para la Paz, Colombia
FORMUJER	Programme for Strengthening the Technical and Vocational Training of Low-income Women
FOSIS	Fondo de Solidaridad e Inversión Social, Chile
FRL	Fondo de Reconversión Laboral, Uruguay

GTZ — Gesellschaft für Technische Zusammenarbeit

HEART/NTA — Human Employment and Resource Training Trust / National Training Agency, Jamaica

ICIC	Instituto de Capacitación de la Industria de la Construcción, Mexico
IDB	Inter-American Development Bank
IILS	International Institute of Labour Studies
ILO	International Labour Organisation
INA	Instituto Nacional de Aprendizaje, Costa Rica
INACAP	Instituto Nacional de Capacitación Profesional, Chile
INAFORP	Instituto Nacional de Formación Profesional, Panamá
INATEC	Instituto Nacional Tecnológico, Nicaragua
INCE	Instituto Nacional de Cooperación Educativa, Venezuela
INET	Instituto Nacional de Educación Tecnológica, Argentina
INFOCAL	Instituto Nacional de Formación y Capacitación Laboral, Bolivia
INFOP	Instituto Nacional de Formación Profesional, Honduras
INFOTEP	Instituto Nacional de Formación Técnico-Profesional, Dominican Republic
INJU	Instituto Nacional de la Juventud, Uruguay
INMETRO	Instituto Nacional de Metrologia, Normalização e Qualidade Industrial, Brazil
INSAFORP	Instituto Salvadoreño de Formación Profesional, El Salvador
INTECAP	Instituto Técnico de Capacitación y Productividad, Guatemala
INTECO	Instituto de Normas Técnicas de Costa Rica

103

JUNAE   Junta Nacional de Empleo de Uruguay

LEAP   Learning for Earning Activities Programme, Jamaica

MINEDUC   Ministerio de Educación de Guatemala

NCTVET   National Council on Technical and Vocational Education and Training
NGO   Non Governmental Organisations
NTA   National Training Agencies

OAS   Organization of American States
OTE   Organismos de Capacitación Autorizados, Chile
OTIR   Organismos Técnicos Intermediarios Reconocidos, Chile

PLANFOR   Plano Nacional de Qualificação do Trabalhador, Brazil
PMJH   Programa de Capacitación Laboral para Mujeres Jefas de Hogar de Chile
POCET   Proyecto en Comayagua de Educación para el Trabajo, Honduras
PRADJAL   Programa Regional de Acciones para el Desarrollo de la Juventud en América Latina
PROJOVEN   Fortalecimiento Integral de Jóvenes en Guatemala (Guatemala)

PROJOVEN   Programa de Capacitación Laboral Juvenil (Peru)
PROJOVEN   Programa de Capacitación e Inserción Laboral de Jóvenes en Uruguay (Uruguay)

SECAP   Servicio Ecuatoriano de Capacitación Profesional
SEFOR   Secretaria de Formação e Desenvolvimento Profissional, Brazil
SEMTEC   Secretaria de Educação Média e Tecnológica, Brazil
SENA   Servicio Nacional de Aprendizaje, Colombia
SENAC   Serviço Nacional de Aprendizagem Comercial, Brazil
SENAI   Serviço Nacional de Aprendizagem Industrial, Brazil
SENAITEC   Centros Nacionais de Tecnologia, Brazil
SENAR   Serviço Nacional de Aprendizagem Rural, Brazil
SENAT   Serviço Nacional de Aprendizagem do Transporte, Brazil
SENATI   Servicio Nacional de Adiestramiento en Trabajo Industrial, Peru
SENCE   Servicio Nacional de Capacitación y Empleo, Chile
SERNAM   Servicio Nacional de la Mujer, Chile
SINE   Sistema Nacional de Evaluación de Costa Rica
SL-TOP   School-Leavers Training Opportunities Programme
SPPE   Secretaria de Políticas Públicas de Emprego, Brazil

TCI   Technology of Communications and Information
TTP   Trayectos Técnicos Profesionales, Argentina
TVET   Technical and Vocational Education and Training

UNDP   United Nations Development Programme
UNESCO   United Nations Educational, Scientific and Cultural Organisation
UNO   United Nations Organisation
UPC   Unidad Promotora de Capacitación, Mexico

VTI   Vocational Training Institutions

WFP   World Food Programme

YTEPP   Youth Training and Employment Partnership Programme, Trinidad and Tobago

400.09.2001

www.ingramcontent.com/pod-product-compliance
Lightning Source LLC
Chambersburg PA
CBHW071520200326
41519CB00019B/6013